LIVING LOW OXALATE COOKBOOK

ULTRA LOW OXALATE RECIPES

MELINDA KEEN

Copyright © 2023 Melinda Keen

All rights reserved. No part of this book may be reproduced by any mechanical or electronic process nor copied for public or private use other than for "fair use" as brief quotations embodied in articles and reviews without prior written permission. The author of this book does not dispense medical advice or prescribe the use of any technique as a form of treatment for physical, emotional, or medical problems without the advice of a physician, either directly or indirectly. The intent of the author is only to offer information of a general nature to help you in your quest for emotional, physical, and spiritual well-being. A health care professional should be consulted regarding your specific situation.

ISBN-9798392939947

Cover Photo by: Melinda Keen
Cover Design: Ryan Matthews
Editor: Jessica Matthews

DEDICATION

This book is dedicated to the Lord my God
who held my hand, gave me strength
when I had none and guided me
out of oxalate related illness.

CONTENTS

Acknowledgments	i
INTRODUCTION	1
BALANCED NUTRITION	11
ULTRA LOW OXALATE FOOD LIST	27
BREADS, CRACKERS AND SNACKS	47
BREAKFAST DISHES	61
SOUPS, SALADS AND DRESSINGS	69
MAIN DISHES	83
SIDE DISHES	122
SMOOTHIES AND DESSERTS	148
About The Author	164
Recipe Title Index	166

ACKNOWLEDGMENTS

I want to give thanks to a loving and supportive husband, Jeff, who witnessed firsthand my journey from chronic illness to health. Thank you for continually encouraging me to share my message of hope and health and my low oxalate recipes with others who may be suffering from oxalate related illness.

INTRODUCTION

This cookbook was written to help others who may struggle from the effects of oxalates in foods you normally consider healthy. Foods such as spinach, beets, sweet potatoes and nuts are some of the most popular foods recommended by health professionals for their high vitamin, mineral, antioxidant and fiber content. These same foods are also very high in a naturally occurring plant compound known as oxalic acid, an anti-nutrient. Oxalates in mild amounts are not a problem for the body as long as the body can safely detoxify each molecule of oxalate. The body has the ability to get rid of oxalates with a healthy digestive system, proper nutrition and with optimal gallbladder function.

    The biggest problem is if one has an inherited rare genetic disorder, such as Primary hyperoxaluria, a condition where the liver doesn't create enough of a certain protein that prevents overproduction of oxalate. Individuals with hyperoxaluria often have persistent calcium oxalate kidney stones which often result in life-threatening kidney stone damage. In general, these rare disorders are identified in childhood. A diagnosis requires genetic testing. Secondary hyperoxaluria is a condition in which excess oxalate is absorbed in the gastrointestinal tract. The reasons for absorption can be due to medical conditions such as inflammatory bowel disease or low counts of oxalate degrading bacterium or simply by over consuming high oxalate foods. My oxalate rich plant-based diet changed me from an active, energetic, physically and emotionally healthy woman to a disabled, exhausted and chronically ill one. My life changed when I discovered how oxalates were responsible for devastating my health. Changing my high oxalate diet to a low oxalate diet was my first step towards healing. The low oxalate diet is also called a renal diet or kidney stone diet. If you've been diagnosed with kidney stones, an autoimmune disorder, neurological disorder, lupus, fibromyalgia or chronic fatigue, experience bladder pain, or suffer with joint pain and inflammation, you should consider the possibility that it may be oxalate related. Unless you've experienced a kidney stone you may not have even heard of oxalates. Unfortunately, kidney stones are not the only health problems that people who regularly consume foods high in oxalates experience. If you're dealing with any type of inflammatory or chronic condition I encourage you to read my previous book *Living Low Oxalate* (2018) to discover what oxalates are, how they impact your health, and the steps necessary to walk away from their influence on chronic disease.

Oxalates are primarily found in plant foods such as vegetables, fruits, grains, legumes, spices, herbs, and almost all nuts and seeds. These molecules are present in the leaves, roots, stems, fruits and seeds. Plants produce this toxic substance to provide a defense against insects and grazing animals. These needle-like crystals tear up the teeth of insects or animals which try to eat them. Most fruits and vegetables contain measurable amounts of oxalates. Some, such as rhubarb, spinach and sweet potatoes have especially high levels. Oxalates in foods are classified as anti-nutrients meaning they interfere with the absorption of vitamins, minerals and other nutrients. They even get in the way of digestive enzymes, which are vital for proper digestion and absorption of nutrients. For this reason a plant-based diet is an unhealthy diet. A low oxalate diet is a meal plan that is low in oxalates and should consist primarily of foods like proteins, dairy products, white rice, and low oxalate fruits and vegetables. It is important to eat a wide variety of foods from the five food groups to ensure that you are consuming all the different nutrients that your body needs. The nutrients in food enables the cells in our bodies to perform their necessary functions. We especially need to pay attention to what we eat when we are ill so we can give our bodies the nutrients it needs to heal. The processed, low-variety foods many people consume regularly may be convenient but they have been shown to compromise our health. Processed food includes food that has been canned, packaged, or changed in nutritional composition with fortifying, preserving, or preparing in different ways. Many contain additives and high amounts of added sugar and sodium.

Eating healthy is not about strict limitations, or eliminating food groups. Every food group has important nutrients, vitamins and minerals that your body needs. Meats, carbohydrates, fats, fruits, vegetables and dairy as close to their natural state as possible is the key to a long healthy life. Another key part of a healthy diet is the absence of toxic chemicals. We should be eating foods that will nourish the body, that are free of residual herbicides, antibiotics, pesticide and hormones. This means cutting out processed foods and replacing them with natural and organic whole foods if there is a choice. Cooking more meals at home can help you take charge of what you're eating and better monitor what's in your food. The recipes in this cookbook are easy to follow; high in key vitamins and minerals, protein, and fiber; and are catered to individuals with oxalate related illness.

An "oxalate-free" diet is near impossible and is not the direction to aim for. Oxalates occur in varying amounts in almost all plant foods. If you eat food, you're almost certainly consuming oxalates in some amount. Typical diets contain upward of 200–300 mg of oxalates per day. Vegetarians tend to consume upwards of 950 mg oxalates per day or more. A low oxalate diet usually calls for less than 50 mg of oxalates per day. The National Kidney Foundation recommends limiting oxalate intake to 40-50 milligrams per day or less. This diet is usually recommended for individuals that have a history of kidney stones or increased levels of oxalic acid in their urine. Sometimes these same calcium oxalate stones form in areas outside of the kidneys causing debilitating muscle and joint pain, inflammation, and chronic conditions such as lupus, arthritis, fibromyalgia, crohn's disease, irritable bowel or bladder and vulvodynia. Oxalate rich foods can interfere with health on a broad systemic level triggering widely varied symptoms such as pain, fatigue, anxiety, inflammation, bladder and gastrointestinal discomfort.

Varied effects of high oxalates in cells and tissues:

* Interferes with and damages mitochondrial function thereby impairing cellular energy
* Creates oxidative stress
* Disrupts mineral absorption and usage
* Depletes nutrients like glutathione and the B vitamins
* Causes histamine release and rashes
* Causes faulty sulfation

Foods with the highest oxalate content (50 mg per serving or higher:

- Almonds
- Hazelnuts
- Peanuts
- Pine nuts
- Poppy seeds
- Sesame seeds
- Beets
- Russet potatoes
- Eggplant
- Spinach
- Swiss chard
- Okra
- Plantain
- Sweet potatoes
- Yams
- Rhubarb

Foods that are very high (30-50 mg. Per serving)

- Chocolate
- Cocoa powder
- Potato chips
- Soy Burger
- Cassava flour
- Wheat flour
- Barley flour
- Bagels
- Apricot
- Hass avocado

- Blackberries
- Raspberries
- Guava
- Kiwi
- Canned black olives
- Pomegranate
- Brown rice
- Celery seeds
- Cinnamon
- Turmeric
- Pinto Beans
- Soy beans
- White beans
- Macadamia nuts
- Pistachio nuts
- Walnuts
- Artichoke hearts
- Bamboo shoots
- Hearts of palm
- Red potatoes
- Rutabaga
- Turnip

A trial on a low oxalate diet (40-50 mg oxalate daily) may put you on the right tract to healing. Withdrawing from some of the highest oxalate rich foods, even for as short as two weeks, can determine whether oxalate influence is at the root of your problem. After two or three weeks, remove more of the highest oxalate foods (above 50 mg per serving). Eliminate and swap out higher oxalate foods for lower ones. Continue lowering your intake a little more each week or two until you average 40-50 mg each day.

After a period of time, I suggest several months, if you have found complete relief of symptoms at this daily amount, this is your maintenance level for health. It's very important to remain on the low oxalate diet. Many people have assumed they no longer have an oxalate issue but this is not a diet one is able to safely stray away from. Eating high oxalate foods will only lead back to high oxalate toxicity and a return of symptoms.

Since many prepackaged snacks, prepared meals and restaurant items have varied and even undetermined amounts of oxalates it can be a little daunting for the low oxalate dieter. Some of the safe snacks are coconut chips, meats, cheeses, pork rinds, caramels, vanilla ice cream, yogurt, white rice crackers and the snack recipes in this book under breads, crackers and snacks.

When eating out the safest choices are meat, fish, seafood and Caesar salads. Shrimp cocktails, chef salads, breakfasts of meats and eggs are also good choices. Water, wine, beer, coffee, apple juice, Ocean Spray cranberry juice and fresh lemonade are the best beverage choices. I create what I call splash waters for variety. It's simply a splash of any fruit juice in your water. Drinking a lot of water is very important on a low oxalate diet. Stored oxalates will be easier to flush from the system.

Once you're familiar with the oxalate content of foods and get past the ups and downs of recovery, you will find living low oxalate easy. You may begin to feel better right away but for most people there comes a time when your body will see this lower oxalate consumption as an opportunity to get rid of any stored oxalates. This is why it's so important to transition into this diet slowly. When oxalate crystals begin to break apart, move out of storage and into your bloodstream, and towards excretion, you may experience a worsening of symptoms. This has been referred to as "dumping" or "crystal shedding". Reducing oxalate levels too quickly can cause the body to dump too much at once which has been known to cause a plethora of symptoms including skin rashes, histamine release, bowel changes, as well as severe issues such as pain, inflammation and possibly kidney stones. Your kidneys can only filter so much at one time. Take time to adjust to each change. The body will gradually break down and remove these toxic crystals. Depending on how fast you can detoxify and how much oxalate you have stored, it could take a few months to possibly a year or more to get your health back.

Most individuals experience great relief of symptoms in a short period of time by lowering oxalates slowly. Yet there are individuals who add back high oxalate foods occasionally and experience a great setback. Thus it takes much longer to find sustained relief. This disrupts the natural healing process. The change from storing oxalates to dumping them can take weeks or even months. You can tell the difference between oxalate induced pain and oxalate dumping pain. Oxalate induced pain, inflammation or swelling occurs quickly after consuming a higher than normal oxalate content food and lasts only a day or two. The body's storage release "dumping" of oxalate causes pain, inflammation and swelling at a lesser intensity and longer duration. There is always a pause, with great relief in symptoms between these two events. I have found that each pause of symptoms is longer in duration.

There are certain individuals who find they must lower their oxalate intake further to find relief. Many times this is due to the amount of oxalobacter formigenes, the oxalate eating bacteria present in the intestinal tract or due to the higher amount of endogenous oxalates produced in the liver. Lowering oxalate intake to 10 mg per day or less is an ultra low oxalate diet. It should not be considered unless you have been on the low oxalate diet for a few years. The dumping by going ultra low oxalate can be quite severe if done quickly. I suggest moving from the low oxalate diet to the ultra low oxalate diet the same way one should transition from a high oxalate diet to the low oxalate diet. Start by removing the higher oxalate foods and adjusting to 25-30 mg of oxalate daily for several weeks before lowering it again to 15-20 mg daily. You will find the ultra low oxalate list in Chapter 3.

The human body has an amazing ability to heal. The process of healing varies with every individual. One factor is the amount of stored oxalates one has to release. Another is how healthy our detoxification pathways are. It's vitally important to nourish the body with vitamin and mineral rich healthy foods.

Several recipes in my previous cookbooks *Low Oxalate Fresh and Fast Cookbook* (2015), *Real Food Real Results* (2016) and *Tame The Flame Cookbook* (2019) are included with modification to be ultra low oxalate.

BALANCED NUTRITION

I believe that choosing foods that are as close to their natural state as possible is the key to a long healthy life. Another key part of a healthy diet is the absence of toxic chemicals. We should be eating foods that will nourish the body like clean, real, pesticide, herbicide and hormone free products. This means cutting out processed foods and replacing them with natural whole foods such as dairy, fruits, vegetables, herbs, meats, fish and eggs. Good fats are also beneficial and should constitute half or more of the calories in a healthy diet.

Dairy

Regardless of whether you opt for raw cows milk, organic lightly pasteurized, or organic pasteurized, the full-fat version is the healthier choice. When the fat is removed from milk, what remains are a significant number of fat-soluble vitamins that can't be absorbed as well as an overabundance of lactose. I use full fat organic dairy products in my recipes because the calcium from dairy binds with oxalates from foods keeping them from being absorbed. Cheese, milk, sour cream, yogurt and buttermilk are all valuable sources of calcium, vitamin D and protein. Dairy contains negligible amounts of oxalate.

Some people with allergies to cow milk may find that goat milk doesn't trigger their allergies. Goat milk is one of the most commonly consumed types of dairy in the world.

Goat milk has more protein, calcium and potassium as well as higher amounts of conjugated linoleic acids that plays important roles in immune stimulation, growth promotion and disease prevention.

Fats

Most of my recipes are made with grass-fed cow's milk butter, ghee, organic unrefined coconut oil and extra-virgin olive oil. Butter, especially from grass-fed cows, is a natural healthy alternative to unnatural and harmful hydrogenated vegetable oils, margarine and shortenings, or genetically modified oils. Rich, creamy, organic grass fed butter is a rich source of vitamins, minerals, antioxidants and healthy fats. Studies have proven that butter helps to prevent heart disease, improves eyesight, balances hormones, strengthens bones and increases nutrient absorption. The incredible supply of Omega 3 fatty acids in butter offers your immune system a boost, which helps to keep it at peak strength to combat colds and flu.

Coconut oil is the healthiest fat for frying and sauteing, because it can withstand high heat without chemically altering. Unrefined coconut oil has the flavor of fresh coconuts since it is not deodorized or chemically processed. It is rich in proteins, vitamins and antioxidants.

Extra-virgin olive oil is a healthy fat to include in your diet if it's not overheated. It should never be used as a frying oil. If the oil is truly extra-virgin it has a distinctive taste and is high in antioxidants. Butter, ghee, coconut oil and olive oil contain negligible amounts of oxalate.

Fruits and Vegetables

It is best to eat fruits and vegetables grown organically, but if budget or availability restricts your choice, remove outer leaves or peels and wash thoroughly. Organic growers are prohibited from using synthetic pesticides and herbicides that have harmful effects on your health. Buy fresh and ripe fruits and vegetables when they are in season. Otherwise, choose frozen. Frozen produce is processed at peak ripeness and is the most nutrient-packed aside from fresh.

My recipes rarely include canned vegetables. For reasons unknown canned vegetables and fruits rate higher in oxalates than the fresh. Another concern is their sodium content, as sodium is often added to help maintain the flavor of vegetables during the canning process. When I do use them, and it's usually because I can't find them fresh or frozen, I rinse them well in a colander. At times, I do choose food in jars, such as jams, simply to save time.

Buying an organic product is important for health and nutrition due to the fact that so many crops are sprayed with glyphosate which is known to produce oxalates in the body. Fruits and vegetables have a wide range of oxalate contents. The recipes in this cookbook do not contain fruits and vegetables in the high oxalate range.

Herbs & Spices

Beyond adding flavor herbs and spices carry unique antioxidants, phytosterols and many other nutrient substances that help our body fight germs and boosts the immune system. Fresh herbs are more readily available during summer months, especially if you grow your own, but some do better when they are dried. Basically, fresh herbs and spices are added near the end of a dish, and dried ones are best added during the cooking so the flavor has time to infuse the whole dish. It is best to choose organic herbs and spices due to the fact that these are plants that are conventionally grown with the use of pesticides. Herbs and spices have a wide range of oxalate contents. The recipes in this cookbook do not contain herbs and spices in the high oxalate range.

Pepper comes from the fruit of the pepper plant. The peppercorns are processed two different ways. Black peppercorns are sun-dried to turn the pepper black. To produce white pepper, the outer layer is removed leaving only the inner seed. The high oxalate content of black pepper comes from the outer layer of the peppercorn. Therefore, white pepper is low in oxalate content and preferred in all of my recipes. If you prefer, small amounts of black pepper can be used in these recipes.

Meat, Fish, and Eggs

Incorporating foods that contain protein can really help to improve your overall health. A high-protein diet increases your muscle mass and strength, lowers blood pressure, aids in weight loss (especially belly fat) and helps you fight diabetes. Protein helps repair and build your body's tissues. It drives metabolic reactions, maintains pH and fluid balance and keeps the immune system strong. It also transports and stores nutrients and can act as an energy source. For optimal health I choose grass-fed organic beef, bison and lamb, pasture-raised turkey and chicken, wild-caught fish and pasture-raised organic eggs. In order to be certified to the US Department of Agriculture's (USDA) organic standards, farms and ranches must follow a strict set of guidelines. The animals' organic feed cannot contain animal by-products, antibiotics or genetically engineered grains and cannot be grown using pesticides or chemical fertilizers. No antibiotics or added growth hormones are allowed, and they must have outdoor access. If you prefer to replace some of the meats with pork I highly recommend you find a naturally raised, pastured source. Pork can have a lot of contaminants.

Farm-raised fish commonly contains high levels of contaminants as well. Farmed fish are fed an unnatural diet of grains and legumes. The healthiest choice is wild-caught fish. These fish tend to be higher in Omega 3 fatty acids, contain very low levels of disease and are free from antibiotics and pesticides.

Eggs are so nutritious that they're often referred to as "nature's multivitamin." Eggs are loaded with vitamins, minerals, high-quality protein, good fats and various other lesser-known nutrients. All meats, fish and eggs contain negligible amounts of oxalate.

Grains

Most of my recipes do not include grains as most grains are high in oxalates. White rice is a gluten-free grain that is low in oxalates, so I add rice to my meals on occasion. The recipes in this cookbook do not contain glutinous grains. Some brands of baking powder use wheat starch to absorb moisture. It's important to choose a brand of baking powder that does not use wheat starch. Rumford and Clabber Girl brands are wheat free and aluminum free as well. Cornstarch is a low oxalate alternative to flour in frying.

Legumes, Nuts and Seeds

Most legumes, nuts and many seeds are extremely high in oxalates. Some lentils, and coconut contain small amounts of oxalate and can be found in many of my recipes.

Vitamins and Minerals

Vitamins and minerals are essential substances that our bodies need to develop and function normally. Most individuals can get all of the necessary vitamins and minerals through a healthy eating pattern of nutrient-dense foods which is highly important for the low oxalate dieter. Important vitamins include A, C, D, E, and K, and the B vitamins: thiamin (B1), riboflavin (B2), niacin (B3), pantothenic acid (B5), pyridoxal (B6), cobalamin (B12), biotin (B7), and folate/folic acid (B9). A number of minerals are essential for health: calcium, phosphorus, potassium, magnesium, iron, zinc, iodine, sulfur, cobalt, copper, manganese and selenium.

Supplements are never a substitute for a balanced healthy diet. People with limited access to healthy food choices or who have certain medical conditions or anyone over the age of 65 may need to focus on adding certain supplements. Unless you take an at-home test or get a blood analysis from your doctor, you don't know if you lack vitamins and need supplements.

Low oxalate sources of vitamin A include:

- Cantaloupe
- Red and yellow bell peppers
- Broccoli
- Brussels sprouts

- Butter
- Cabbage
- Egg
- Romaine
- Acorn and spaghetti squash

Low oxalate sources of vitamin C include:

- Lemon juice
- Green peas
- Bok choy
- Red bell pepper
- Romaine
- Cantaloupe
- Apple
- Green grapes

Low oxalate sources of vitamin D include:

- Sardines
- Salmon
- Trout
- Egg

Your body also makes vitamin D when direct sunlight converts a chemical in your skin into an active form of the vitamin (calciferol).

Low oxalate sources of vitamin E include:

- Coconut oil
- Egg
- Cod

- Trout
- Salmon
- Chicken
- Milk
- Butter
- Cheese

Low oxalate sources of vitamin K include:

- Romaine
- Brussels sprouts
- Cabbage
- Cauliflower
- Egg
- Pork
- Chicken
- Cheese
- Beef
- Butter
- Milk

Low oxalate sources of vitamin B1 (Thiamin) include:

- Egg
- Cauliflower
- Pork
- Trout
- Beef
- Salmon
- Oysters

Low oxalate sources of vitamin B2 (Riboflavin) include:

- Pork
- Beef
- Lamb
- Fish
- Egg
- Dairy

Low oxalate sources of vitamin B3 (Niacin) include:

- Fish
- Chicken
- Turkey
- Pork
- Beef
- Salmon
- Mushrooms
- Green peas

Low oxalate sources of vitamin B5 (pantothenic acid) include:

- Egg
- Milk
- Yogurt
- Salmon
- Shellfish
- Organ meats

Low oxalate sources of vitamin B6 (Pyridoxal) include:

- Beef
- Pork
- Lamb
- Chicken
- Turkey
- Salmon
- Egg
- Banana
- Milk
- Cottage cheese
- White rice
- Onion
- Winter squash

Low oxalate sources of vitamin B12 (Cobalamin) include:

- Clams
- Trout
- Salmon
- Beef
- Pork
- Chicken
- Egg
- Yogurt

Low oxalate sources of vitamin B7 (Biotin) include:

- Milk
- Yogurt
- Cheese

- Egg
- Salmon
- Sardines
- Pork
- Beef
- Mushrooms
- Cauliflower
- Bananas

Low oxalate sources of vitamin B9 (folate/folic acid) include:

- Egg
- Lamb
- Shellfish
- Salmon
- Yogurt
- Black-eyed peas
- Brussels Sprouts
- Lettuce
- Broccoli
- Rice
- Lemon

Low oxalate sources of Calcium include:

- Dairy
- Sardines
- Salmon

Low oxalate sources of Phosphorus include:

- Chicken
- Turkey
- Pork
- Organ Meats
- Seafood
- Dairy

Low oxalate sources of Potassium include:

- Egg
- Pork
- Beef
- Shrimp
- Rice
- Bananas
- Cantaloupe
- Mushrooms
- Cucumber
- Yogurt
- Trout
- Cod

Low oxalate sources of Magnesium include:

- Pumpkin Seeds
- Fish
- Bananas
- Milk
- Yogurt
- Green peas

Note: Food sources of magnesium are limited on a low oxalate diet. It is often necessary to supplement magnesium in order to meet the minimum daily requirement. For adults 19-51+ years the minimum requirement is 400-420 mg daily for men and 310-320 mg for women. Magnesium activates over 300 enzyme reactions in the body, translating to thousands of biochemical reactions happening on a constant basis daily. Magnesium is crucial to nerve transmission, muscle contraction, blood coagulation, energy production, nutrient metabolism bone and cell formation. Magnesium also binds with oxalate in the intestine and in urine which reduces oxalate absorption and stops oxalate from binding with calcium to form kidney stones.

Low oxalate sources of Iron include:

- Beef
- Chicken
- Lamb
- Pork
- Veal
- Shellfish
- Sardines
- Egg

Low oxalate sources of Zinc include:

- Seafood
- Beef
- Chicken
- Pork
- Yogurt

Low oxalate sources of Iodine include:

- Egg
- Dairy
- Cod
- Shrimp

Low oxalate sources of Sulfur include:

- Egg
- Brussels sprouts
- Cauliflower
- Bok choy
- Garlic
- Onion

Low oxalate sources of Cobalt include:

- Fish and shellfish
- Organ meats
- Beef
- Milk

Low oxalate sources of Copper include:

- Seafood
- Meats
- Egg
- Mushrooms

Low oxalate sources of Manganese include:

- Shellfish
- Chickpeas

Low oxalate sources of Selenium include:

- Seafood
- Pork
- Beef
- Turkey
- Chicken
- Egg
- Dairy
- Banana

ULTRA LOW OXALATE FOOD LISTS

If you are advised to follow a low oxalate diet, the first thing you will want is a reliable list of foods and their oxalate content. An Internet search for oxalate content of foods lists will result in numerous lists that are conflicting. It is impossible to compile a comprehensive food list with oxalate values due to the enormous amount and variety of foods. For example, there are 2,500 varieties of apples grown the United States. Oxalate content in plants can also vary due to differences in climate they were grown and the soil they were grown in. All of these issues can be very discouraging for the individual wishing to follow a low oxalate diet.

Dr. Penniston and colleagues at the University of Wisconsin compared the data reported on a publicly available database of food oxalate content (maintained by the Harvard University School of Public Health) with values from the Nutrition Data System for Research, a nutrient analysis software program. The data on the website provide information for 536 foods analyzed using liquid chromatography, which is considered the gold-standard, state-of-the-art method for oxalate analysis.

Another very lengthy oxalate content list comes from the VP Foundation. The VP Foundation began advocating research for a 21st century low oxalate diet during the early 1990's, and started an Oxalate Testing Fund for Foods and Beverages in 1995 in collaboration with the University of Wyoming. Currently, the VP Foundation is completing a longstanding project to retest hundreds of foods for soluble oxalate content. Joining the VP Foundation entitles you to the foundation newsletter published twice a year that lists oxalate testing results, recipe ideas and related news. Find information online at https://www.thevpfoundation.org.

I highly recommend joining a private group on Facebook called Trying Low Oxalates (TLO) for knowledgeable support, oxalate related PubMed articles, and access to a comprehensive Low Oxalate Spreadsheet.

The following low oxalate foods lists include Harvard's low oxalate foods list as well as the VP Foundation Newsletter additions. I've reduced these extensive lists down to items less than 20 mg oxalate values to shorten the lists. Where an oxalate list shows a value of 20 mg and you wish to make it an addition to your ultra low oxalate diet simply halve the serving size. The oxalate content values in the recipes are calculated first by using the more up-to-date VP Foundation oxalate foods list. If the food item isn't listed there, the values come from the Harvard oxalate food list.

HARVARD OXALATE FOOD LIST
(Ultra low oxalate)

Food Group	Serving size	Oxalate Value
Fruits		
Whole Fruits		
Avocados	1 fruit	19 mg
Grapefruit	1/2 fruit	12 mg
Tangerine	1 fruit	10 mg
Figs	1 medium fig	9 mg
Apple Sauce	1 cup	2 mg
Banana	1 fruit	3 mg
Blackberries	1/2 cup	2 mg
Blueberries	1/2 cup	2 mg
Cherries	1 cup	3 mg

Food Group	Serving size	Oxalate Value
Limes	1/2 fruit	3 mg
Pears	1 fruit	2 mg
Pineapple	1 cup	4 mg
Strawberries	1/2 cup	2 mg
Raisins	1 oz	3 mg
Apples	1 fruit	1 mg
Apricots	1 fruit	0 mg
Cantaloupe	1/4 melon	1 mg
Grapes	½ cup	1 mg
Honeydew	1 cup	1 mg
Lemons	1 wedge	1 mg
Mango	1 fruit	1 mg
Nectarine	1 fruit	0 mg
Papaya	1 medium fruit	1 mg
Peaches	1 fruit	0 mg
Plantain	1 medium	1 mg
Plums	1 fruit	0 mg
Watermelon	1 slice	1 mg

Canned Fruits

Canned Cherries	1/2 cup	7 mg
Cranberry Sauce	1/2 cup	2 mg
Canned Pears	1/2 cup	1 mg
Canned Peaches	1/2 cup	1 mg
Fruit Cocktail	1/2 cup	1 mg

Dried Fruits

Dried Prunes	¼ cup	11 mg
Dried Apples	1 cup	2 mg
Dried Apricots	1 cup	3 mg
Dried Cranberries	1/2 cup	1 mg

Vegetables

Olives	8-12 olives	18 mg
Parsnip	1/2 cup	15 mg
Kidney Beans	1/2 cup	15 mg
Refried Beans	1/2 cup	16 mg
Tomato Sauce	1/2 cup	17 mg
Carrots, raw	1/2 lg.	10 mg
Celery, cooked	1 cup	10 mg
Collards	1 cup	10 mg
Artichokes	1 small	5 mg
Asparagus	4 spears	6 mg
Carrots, cooked	1/2 cup	7 mg
Hot Chili Pepper	1/2 cup	5 mg
Mixed Vegetables, frozen	1/2 cup	5 mg
Oriental Vegetables, frozen	1/2 cup	6 mg
Soybeans	1 cup	7 mg
String Beans	1/2 cup	9 mg
Tomato	1 med	7 mg

Food Group	Serving size	Oxalate Value
Brussels Sprouts	1/2 cup	2 mg
Celery, raw	1 stalk	3 mg
Kale, chopped	1 cup	2 mg
Mung Beans	1/2 cup	3 mg
Mustard Greens	1 cup chopped	4 mg
Sea Vegetables	1 cup	3 mg
Alfalfa Sprouts	1/2 cup	0 mg
Bok Choy	1 cup, raw	1 mg
Broccoli, chopped	1/2 cup	1 mg
Cabbage	1/2 cup	1 mg
Cauliflower, cooked	1/2 cup	1 mg
Chives	1 tsp.	0 mg
Corn	1/2 cup	1 mg
Cucumber	1/4 cucumber	1 mg
Endive	1/2 cup	0 mg
Green Pepper	1 ring	1 mg
Iceberg Lettuce	1 cup	0 mg
Mushrooms	1 mushroom	0 mg
Onions	1 small onion	0 mg
Peas	1/2 cup	1 mg
Pickles	1 pickle	0 mg
Radish	10 count	0 mg
Romaine Lettuce	1 cup	0 mg
Scallions	1/2 cup	1 mg
Sauerkraut	1/2 cup	1 mg
Water Chestnuts	4 chestnuts	0 mg
Yellow Squash	1/2 cup	1 mg
Zucchini	1/2 cup	1 mg
Potato Salad	1/3 cup	17 mg

Dairy

Cream Products

Homemade Cream Sauce	1 cup	3 mg
Coffee Creamer	1 tbsp.	0 mg
Non-Dairy Creamer	1 tbsp.	0 mg
Sour Cream	1 tbsp.	0 mg

Ice Creams

Ice Cream, vanilla	1/2 cup	0 mg
Ice Cream, light	1/2 cup	0 mg
non fat Ice Cream	1/2 cup	0 mg

Yogurt

Plain Yogurt	1 cup	2 mg
Yogurt with Fruit	8 oz	1 mg
Frozen Yogurt	1/2 cup	1 mg

Food Group	Serving size	Oxalate Value
Low Fat Frozen Yogurt	1/2 cup	1 mg

Cheese

American Cheese	1 slice	0 mg
Cheddar Cheese	1 slice	0 mg
Low Fat Cheese	1 slice	0 mg
Cottage Cheese	1/2 cup	0 mg
Low Fat Cottage Cheese	1 cup	0 mg
Fat Free Cottage Cheese	1/2 cup	1 mg
Mozzarella	1 oz	0 mg
Egg	1 medium	0 mg
Egg Beaters	4 oz	0 mg

Dairy Spreads

Cream Cheese	1 oz	0 mg
Cream Cheese, fat free	1 oz	1 mg
Low Fat Cream Cheese	1 oz	1 mg
Butter, salted	1 pat	0 mg

Milk

Chocolate Milk	1 cup	7 mg
Powdered Milk	1 envelope	3 mg
Fat Free Milk	1 cup	1 mg
1% Milk	1 cup	1 mg
2% Milk	1 cup	1 mg
Whole Milk	1 cup	1 mg
Buttermilk	1 cup	1 mg

Breads & Grains

Breads

French Toast	2 slices	13 mg
English Muffin, Whole Wheat	1 muffin	12 mg
Pancakes, homemade	4 cakes	11 mg
Pancakes (mix)	4 cakes	10 mg
Blueberry Muffins	1 muffin	9 mg
Biscuits, plain or buttermilk	1 biscuit	6 mg
Bran Muffins	1 muffin	5 mg
Bran Muffin, low fat	1 muffin	5 mg
Cracked Wheat Bread	1 slice	5 mg
English Muffin	1 muffin	8 mg
English Muffin, whole grain	1 muffin	8 mg

Food Group	Serving size	Oxalate Value
Wheat	1 muffin	7 mg
Low Fat Muffins	1 muffin	5 mg
Rye Bread	1 slice	7 mg
Tortillas, Corn	1 tortilla	7 mg
Tortillas, Flour	1 tortilla	8 mg
White Bread	1 slice	5 mg
Wheat Bran Bread	1 slice	7 mg
Whole Oat Bread	1 slice	5 mg
Whole Wheat Bread	1 slice	6 mg
Corn Bread	1 piece	4 mg
Oatmeal Bread	1 piece	4 mg
Oat Bran Muffin	1 small muffin	4 mg
Oat Bran Bread	1 slice	4 mg

Pastas, Rice & Grains

Flour, All-Purpose	1 cup	17 mg
Couscous	1 cup	15 mg
Spaghetti	1 cup cooked	11 mg
White Rice Flour	1 cup	11 mg
Corn Flour	1 cup	3 mg
Hummus	1 tbsp.	4 mg
Macaroni & Cheese	1 cup	4 mg
White Rice, cooked	1 cup	4 mg
Flour, Barley Malt	1 cup	0 mg
Corn Bran	1 cup	0 mg
Flaxseed	1 tbsp.	0 mg
Oat Bran, raw	1/3 cup	0 mg

Meats & Fish

Meat and Meat Alternatives

Soy Burger	3.5 oz	12 mg
Chicken Nuggets	6 nuggets	3 mg
Meatballs	2 meatballs	2 mg
Turkey Dogs	1 dog	3 mg
Antelope	3 oz	0 mg
Bacon	2 slices	0 mg
Bologna	1 slice	0 mg
Buffalo	3 oz	0 mg
Chicken Dog	1 dog	1 mg
Chicken Liver	3 oz	0 mg
Chicken	3 oz	0 mg
Hot Dogs	1 dog	1 mg
Ham	3 oz	0 mg
Ground Beef	3 oz	0 mg

Food Group	Serving size	Oxalate Value
Hamburger, lean (85%)	3 oz	0 mg
Hamburger, Lean (75%)	3 oz	0 mg
Hamburger, lean (90%)	3 oz	1 mg
Liver	3.5 oz	0 mg
Moose	3 oz	0 mg
Pork	5 oz	0 mg
Turkey	5 oz	0 mg
Venison	3 oz	0 mg
Wild Game Meat	3 oz	1 mg

Fish

Tuna Salad	1 cup	6 mg
Fish Sticks, frozen	2 sticks	3 mg
Crab, Alaskan King	3 oz	0 mg
Bluefish	1 fillet	1 mg
Clams, raw	3 oz	0 mg
Cod, Pacific	1 fillet	0 mg
Cod Liver, Fish Oil	1 tsp.	0 mg
Flounder	3 oz	0 mg
Haddock	3 oz	0 mg
Halibut	3 oz	0 mg
Herring, Atlantic & Pacific	3 oz	1 mg
Mackerel	3 oz	0 mg
Oysters	3 oz	0 mg
Pollock	3 oz	0 mg
Salmon all types	4 oz	0 mg
Sardines	3.75 oz	0 mg
Shrimp	3 oz	0 mg
Swordfish	1 piece	0 mg
Tuna Fish, in oil	3.5 oz	0 mg
Tuna Fish, in water	3.5 oz	0 mg
Whiting	3 oz	0 mg

Nuts and Seeds

Pistachios	1 oz	14 mg
Pumpkin Seeds	1 cup, cooked	17 mg
Pecans	1 oz	10 mg
Sunflower Seeds	1 cup	12 mg
Flaxseed	1 tbsp.	0 mg

Food Group	Serving size	Oxalate Value
Cakes, Candies, Cookies & Pudding Snack		
Cake, store brand	1 piece	15 mg
Cake, homemade	1 piece	16 mg
Cake, low fat only	1 piece	11 mg
Chocolate Chip Cookie	1 cookie	10 mg
Milk Chocolate Candies	1 oz	5 mg
Apple Pie	1(1/8th) piece	5 mg
Pudding Popsicle	1 popsicle	5 mg
Fig Bars	1 cookie	4 mg
Chocolate Pudding, Instant	1 oz or 1/4 box	4 mg
Oatmeal Cookies	1 cookie	4 mg
Rice Cake	1 cake	4 mg
Rice Pudding	1/2 cup	2 mg
Snack Cakes, crème filled	1 cake	3 mg
Custard	1 cup	1 mg
Jell-O	1 cup	1 mg
Popsicle	1 stick	0 mg
Rice Krispy Treat	1 bar	1 mg
Sherbet	1/2 cup	0 mg
Tapioca Pudding	1/2 cup	0 mg
Vanilla Pudding	1 cup	1 mg
Crackers, Chips and Miscellaneous		
Tortilla Corn Chips	1 oz	7 mg
Popcorn, oil-popped	1 cup	5 mg
Pretzels, hard salted	1 oz	5 mg
Fruit Roll-Ups	1 roll	2 mg
Graham Crackers	1 large	2 mg
Popcorn, air-popped	1 cup	4 mg
Ritz Crackers	5 crackers	3 mg
Saltines	1 cracker	1 mg
Triscuits	1 cracker	1 mg
Wheat Crackers	1 cracker	1 mg
Wheat Thins, Reduced Fat	1 cracker	1 mg
Beverages		
Lemonade, frozen concentrate	8 oz	15 mg
Rice Dream	1 cup	13 mg
Tea, brewed	1 cup	14 mg
Tomato Juice	1 cup	14 mg

Food Group	Serving size	Oxalate Value
V8 Juice	1 cup	18 mg
Prune Juice	1 cup	7 mg
Apple Juice	6 oz	2 mg
Apricot Juice	1 cup	2 mg
Coffee, decaff	1 cup	2 mg
Orange Juice	1 cup	2 mg
Pineapple Juice	8 oz	3 mg
Coffee Substitute	1 serving	2 mg
Coffee	1 cup	1 mg
Gatorade	1 cup	0 mg
Grape Juice	8 oz	1 mg
Grapefruit Juice	8 oz	0 mg
Kool-Aid	1 cup	1 mg
Lemonade, diet	8 oz	1 mg
Mango Juice	8 oz	1 mg
Sodas (all types)	8 oz	0 mg
Sweetened Instant Iced Tea	1 cup	0 mg
Water	8 oz	0 mg
Dairy Beverages		
Chocolate Milk	1 cup	7 mg
Powdered Milk	1 envelope	3 mg
Soy Milk	1 cup	4 mg
Fat Free Milk	1 cup	1 mg
1% Milk	1 cup	1 mg
2% Milk	1 cup	1 mg
Whole Milk	1 cup	1 mg
Alcoholic Beverages		
Beer, regular	1 can	4 mg
Red Wine	4 oz	1 mg
Beer, light	1 can	3 mg
White Wine	4 oz	0 mg
Liquor 80 proof	1 jigger	0 mg
Spread, Sauces & Toppings		
Peanut Butter	1 tbsp.	13 mg
Peanut Butter, Reduced fat	1 tbsp.	16 mg
Tahini	1 tbsp.	16 mg
Cream Sauce	1 cup	3 mg
Gravy	1 cup	4 mg
Soy Sauce	1 tbsp.	3 mg
Apple Butter	1 tbsp.	0 mg
Butter	1 pat	0 mg
Catsup/Ketchup	1 packet	1 mg
Cream Cheese	1 oz	0 mg

Food Group	Serving size	Oxalate Value
Cream Cheese, low fat	1 oz	1 mg
Cream Cheese, fat free	1 oz	1 mg
Horseradish	1 tbsp.	0 mg
Jam/Jelly	1 tbsp.	1 mg
Italian Salad Dressing	1 tbsp.	0 mg
Mayonnaise	1 tbsp.	0 mg
Mustard, yellow	1 tsp.	1 mg
Pancake Syrup	3/4 tbsp.	0 mg
Salsa	1 tbsp.	1 mg
Whipped Cream	2 tbsp.	0 mg
Whipped Topping	2 tbsp.	0 mg

Flour and Baking

Flour, All-Purpose	1 cup	17 mg
Flour, White Rice	1 cup	11 mg
Chili Powder	1 tbsp.	7 mg
Brewer's Yeast	1 tbsp.	7 mg
Corn Flour	1 cup	3 mg
Cornstarch	1 cup	3 mg
Lemon Juice, can or bottle	1 cup	4 mg
Artificial Sweetener	1 packet	1 mg
Bouillon Cube	1 cube	1 mg
Black Pepper	1 dash	0 mg
Flour, Barley Malt	1 cup	0 mg
Brown Sugar	1 cup packed	1 mg
Butter	1 pat	0 mg
Buttermilk	1 cup	1 mg
Corn Syrup, high fructose	1 tbsp.	1 mg
Corn Syrup, Light	1 tbsp.	0 mg
Cod Liver Oil	1 tsp.	0 mg
Cream Substitute	1 tsp.	0 mg
Cream	1 tbsp.	0 mg
Egg	1 medium egg	0 mg
Eggbeaters	4 oz	0 mg
Garlic Powder	1 tsp.	0 mg
Gelatin	1 tbsp.	0 mg
Honey	1 tbsp.	0 mg
Lard	1 tsp.	0 mg
Lemon Juice, raw	1 tbsp.	0 mg
Molasses	1 tbsp.	0 mg
Oat Flour	1 cup	0 mg
Salt	1 tsp.	0 mg
Shortening	1 tsp.	0 mg
Sugar	1 tsp.	0 mg
Sweet Whey, fluid	1 cup	1 mg

Food Group	Serving size	Oxalate Value
Fast Food Items or Meals		
Cheeseburger, with bun	1 burger	13 mg
Burritos, with beans	1 burrito	17 mg
Burritos, with beans & meat	1 burrito	16 mg
Enchilada, beef & cheese	1 enchilada	13 mg
Enchilada, with chicken	1 enchilada	13 mg
Lasagna, with meat	1 serving	23 mg
Nachos, with cheese	6-8 chips	13 mg
Cheese Pizza	2 slices	13 mg
Grilled Cheese	1 sandwich	12 mg
Tacos	1 small taco	12 mg
Doughnut	1 doughnut	5 mg
Eggroll	1	5 mg
Hot Dog, with bun	1 dog with bun	9 mg
Onion Rings	6-8 rings	5 mg
Chicken Nuggets	6 nuggets	3 mg
Macaroni & Cheese	1 cup	4 mg
Chicken Roll	1 package	1 mg
Soups		
Clam Chowder	1 cup	13 mg
Vegetable Beef Soup	1 cup	5 mg
Chicken Noodle Soup	1 can	3 mg
Breakfast Items		
Cream of Wheat	1 cup	18 mg
Red River Cereal	1/4 cup	13 mg
Farina Cereal	1 cup	16 mg
French Toast	2 slices	13 mg
Danish Pastry, homemade	1 pastry	14 mg
Sweet Rolls, low fat	1 pastry	13 mg
English Muffins, whole wheat	1 muffin	12 mg
Bran Muffins	1 muffin	5 mg
Bran Muffin low fat	1 muffin	5 mg
Muffin, blueberry	1 muffin	9 mg
Doughnut	1 doughnut	5 mg

Food Group	Serving size	Oxalate Value
English Muffins	1 muffin	8 mg
English Muffins, multi-grain	1 muffin	8 mg
English Muffins, wheat	1 muffin	7 mg
Muffins, low fat	1 muffin	5 mg
Poptart	1 tart	7 mg
Cornbread	1 piece	4 mg
Danish Pastry, fruit filled	1 pastry	4 mg
Granola Bars, low fat	1 oz uncoated	2 mg
Kashi Go Lean Bar	1 bar	3 mg
Carnation Instant Breakfast	1 packet	1 mg
Bacon	2 slices	0 mg
Eggs	1 medium egg	0 mg
Eggbeaters	4 oz	0 mg
Granola Bars, hard & plain	1 bar	1 mg
Oatmeal Cereal	1 cup	0 mg
Pancake Syrup	3/4 tbsp.	0 mg

Cereals by Manufacturer

Kellogg's

All-Bran Buds	1/2 cup	20 mg
Complete Bran	3/4 cup	15 mg
Just Right Fruit & Nut	1 cup	13 mg
Low Fat Granola, with Raisins	2/3 cup	16 mg
Kashi Go Lean	3/4 cup	14 mg
Mueslix Apple & Almond	2/3 cup	20 mg
Mueslix	2/3 cup	17 mg
Puffed Kashi	1 cup	13 mg
Smart Start	1 cup	15 mg
All-Bran with extra fiber	1/2 cup	11 mg
Cocoa Krispies	3/4 cup	11 mg
Kashi Good Friends	3/4 cup	10 mg
Complete Oat Bran Flakes	3/4 cup	5 mg
Kashi Heart to Heart	3/4 cup	8 mg
Healthy Choice, multi-grain	3/4 cup	7 mg
Froot Loops	1 cup	2 mg
Rice Krispies	1 1/4 cup	4 mg

Food Group	Serving size	Oxalate Value
Honey Crunch Corn Flakes	3/4 cup	3 mg
Special K	1 cup	3 mg
Special K Red Berries	1 cup	2 mg
Smacks	3/4 cup	3 mg
Corn Flakes	1 cup	1 mg
Corn Pops	1 cup	1 mg
Crispix	1 cup	1 mg
Frosted Flakes	3/4 cup	1 mg
Product 19	1 cup	1 mg
Post Cereals		
Great Grains Raisin, Dates, Pecans	1 cup	17 mg
Grape Nuts	1/2 cup	14 mg
Blueberry Morning	1/2 cup	8 mg
Grape Nuts Flakes	3/4 cup	7 mg
Fruity Pebbles	3/4 cup	2 mg
Honeycomb	1 1/3 cup	1 mg
Wafflecrisp	1 cup	1 mg
General Mills		
Basic 4	1 cup	17 mg
Fiber One	1/2 cup	13 mg
Nature Valley Cinnamon Raisin Granola	3/4 cup	13 mg
Oatmeal Raisin Crisp	1 cup	13 mg
Harmony	1 1/4 cup	11 mg
Wheaties Raisin Bran	1 cup	11 mg
Apple Cinnamon Cheerios	3/4 cup	5 mg
Berry Bust Cheerios	1 cup	7 mg
Cheerios	1 cup	8 mg
Cinnamon Toast Crunch	3/4 cup	5 mg
Corn Chex	1 cup	5 mg
Count Chocula	1 cup	5 mg
Frosted Cheerios	1 cup	6 mg
Honey Nut Cheerios	1 cup	7 mg
Golden Grahams	3/4 cup	9 mg
Lucky Charms	1 cup	5 mg
Reese's Puffs	3/4 cup	8 mg
Team Cheerios	1 cup	6 mg
Total Corn Flakes	1 1/3 cup	5 mg

Food Group	Serving size	Oxalate Value
Wheat Chex	1 cup	7 mg
Wheaties	1 cup	8 mg
Whole Grain Total	3/4 cup	8 mg
Cocoa Puffs	1 cup	3 mg
Kix	1 1/3 cup	2 mg
Rice Chex	1 1/4 cup	4 mg
Trix	1 cup	0 mg

Quaker

Low Fat 100% Natural Granola with Raisins	3/4 cup	15 mg
100% Natural Granola Oats and Honey	1/2 cup	13 mg
Oat Bran	1 1/4 cup	10 mg
Honey Nut Oats	1 oz	7 mg
Oatmeal Squares	1 cup	5 mg
Puffed Wheat	1 1/4 cup	9 mg
Toasted Oatmeal	1 oz	6 mg
Puffed Rice	1 cup	2 mg
Qaker Oat Cinnamon Life	3/4 cup	3 mg
Quaker Oat Life	3/4 cup	3 mg
Cap'n Crunch	3/4 cup	0 mg

Other Cereal Brands

Uncle Sam	1 cup	11 mg
Just Right with Crunchy Nuggets	1 cup	5 mg
Wheetabix Whole Wheat	2 biscuits	8 mg
Healthy Valley Oat Bran Flakes	1 cup	0 mg

THE VP FOUNDATION OXALATE LIST
(Ultra Low Oxalate Foods)

Food Group	Serving size	Oxalate Value
Baking Items and Grains		
Baking Powder	1 tsp	0.11
Cream of Tartar	1 tsp	1.05
Honey, Clover, Madhava Mountain Gold	1 tbsp	1.39
Maple Syrup, pure	1 tbsp	0.66
Sugar, Coconut sugar, Organic	1 tsp	0.77
Yeast, active dry, Fleishmann's	1 tbsp	4.00

Food Group	Serving size	Oxalate Value
Pure Chocolate extract	1 tsp	0.27
Flour, Coconut, Bob's Red Mill (GF)	1/4 cup	2.21
Corn, Cornstarch, Argo	1 tsp	0.08
Cowpea Bean Flour (Black-Eyed Pea Flour)	1/2 cup	3.80
Flax seed, ground, unspecified brand (GF)	1 tbsp	0.50
Flour, Garbanzo Bean, (Chickpea), Bob's Red Mill (GF)	1/4 cup	2.28
Flour Oat, Bob's Red Mill,	1/4 cup	7.99
Flour, Potato Starch, Bob's Red Mill	1/4 cup	1.34
Flour, Rice, Brown, Organic, Arrowhead Mills	1/4 cup	5.63
Tapioca Flour, Bob's Red Mill	1/4 cup	9.43
Flour, Water Chestnut, unspecified brand	1/2 cup	3.65
Aromatic Jasmine Rice	1/4 cup dry	1.98
Plain Tortillas, (GF), Udi's	1 tortilla	3.32
Grain, Corn, Sweet, fresh,	1/2 cup	0.69
Organic Popcorn, Himalayan Pink Salt, Lesser Evil, Popcorn	1 bag	2.87
Pasta, Noodles, Rice, Thai Kitchen	1/2 cup cooked	1.85

Beverages

Gatorade, Lemon-Lime	12 oz	0.00
Juice, Apple	1 cup	2.23
Juice, Cranberry, 100%, Ocean Spray	1 cup	1.92
Juice, Cranberry, no brand specified	1 cup	1.01
Juice, Grapefruit, bottled, no brand specified	1 cup	0.25
Juice, Lemon, no brand specified	1 tbsp	0.09
Juice, Lime, no brand specified	1 cup	4.51
Juice, Orange, bottled, Schweppes	1 cup	1.25
Juice, Orange, no brand specified	1 cup	0.50
Juice, Orange, pulp free, Juice, Simply Orange	1 cup	0.24
Juice, Red Grape, no brand specified	1 cup	5.25
Juice, Pineapple, Dole	1 cup	2.88

Crackers and Snacks

Pretzel Crisps, Original Snack Factory	14 crackers	0.70
Celtic Sea Salt Caramels	4 caramels	0.00

Food Group	Serving size	Oxalate Value
Apple, Apple Sauce, unsweetened, Eden Organic	1/2 cup	1.10
Apple, Apple Sauce, Vermont Village	1/2 cup	3.25
Apple, Bramleys	1	4.14
Apple, Cox Kent	1	1.38
Apple, Fuji, small	1	3.87
Apple, Gala, medium	1	2.73
Apple, Golden Delicious	1	2.91
Apple, Granny Smith, medium	1	4.83
Apple, Macintosh, medium	1	5.28
Apple, Pink Lady	1	2.88
Apple, Pink Lady, Organic	1	1.97
Apple, Red	1	2.62
Avocado, Hass, La Huerta, Moderately-ripe (+2 days)	1 medium	6.90
Banana (moderately ripe), Dole	1 medium	5.41
Berries, Blueberries	1/2 cup	4.03
Berries, Raspberries, raw	1/2 cup	11.62
Berries, Cranberries, dried, Craisins, Ocean Spray	1/4 cup	2.88
Berries, Cranberries, dried	1/2 cup	1.44
Cherries, Sweet, raw	1/2 cup	1.18
Cherry, Black	1/2 cup	4.60
Cherry, Red	1/2 cup	7.25
Grapes, Concord	1/2 cup	3.45
Grapes, Red, Seedless	1/2 cup	2.00
Grapes, Thompson Seedless, (green),	1 cup	1.36
Mango, raw, fresh	1	3.31
Melons, Cantaloupe, cubed	1/2 cup	3.04
Melons, Watermelon, raw, diced	1/2 cup	0.23
Nectarine, fresh	1 fruit	1.55
Olives, canned, black,	1 medium	0.53
Orange, Navel	1	3.08
Peach, raw (2 1/2 in diameter)	1	2.45
Pear, Bartlett, raw, peeled	1/2 cup	3.05
Pineapple	1/2 cup	4.21
Plum, Yellow, raw	1	0.92
Raisins, Mini Snacks, Sun-Maid	1 box	2.15

Vegetables and Legumes

Pure canned pumpkin, Libby's	½ cup	1.83
Asparagus, boiled	1/2 cup	2.34
Baby, Bok Choy, raw	1 cup	1.58
Bok Choy, leaves	1/2 cup	2.05
Bok Choy, stalks, diced	1/2 cup	0.66
Broccoli florets, boiled, 12 min	1/2 cup	1.08
Brussel Sprouts, boiled	1/2 cup	0.90
Cabbage, green, raw, shredded	1/2 cup	1.80
Cabbage, Napa, chopped	1 cup	2.76
Cabbage, Savoy, shredded	1/2 cup	2.63
Cauliflower, boiled 10 min	1/2 cup	1.36

Food Group	Serving size	Oxalate Value
Cauliflower, raw	1/2 cup	0.20
Cucumbers, raw, sliced	1/2 cup	0.24
Greens, Arugula (rocket)	1/2 cup	0.71
Greens, Kale, Green, raw, chopped	1/2 cup	4.05
Greens, Mustard Greens, boiled	1/2 cup	3.15
Greens, Turnip, boiled 6 min.	1/2 cup	4.75
Lettuce, Bibb, chopped	1/2 cup	2.52
Lettuce, Boston, shredded	1/2 cup	1.18
Lettuce, Iceberg, raw, shredded	1 cup	2.02
Lettuce, Romaine, shredded	1/2 cup	0.45
Mushrooms, canned	1/2 cup	0.55
Mushrooms, Portabella, chopped	1/2 cup	2.75
Mushrooms, Shiitake, fresh	1 piece	0.74
Onion, Yellow, 1 medium	1 medium	1.87
Pepper, Sweet, Red, chopped	1/2 cup	1.79
Seaweed, Nori Sheets	1 sheet	3.53
Shallots, chopped	1/2 cup	1.16
Spaghetti Squash, raw	1 cup	1.82
Squash, Acorn, baked, cubed	1/2 cup	3.09
Squash, Butternut, baked	1/2 cup	4.90
Squash, Yellow, fresh sliced	1/2 cup	3.87
Squash, Zucchini, raw, sliced	1/2 cup	3.25
Tomato Paste, Hunt's	1 tsp	1.34
Tomato, Big Beef, sliced	1/2 cup	4.05
Tomato, Cherry (Peacevine)	1	0.57
Turnip root, steamed 15 min	1/2 cup	2.70
Water Chestnuts, canned, sliced	1/2 cup	2.45
Black-eyed Peas, dried, cooked	1/2 cup, cooked	0.88
Black-Eyed Peas, canned, Whole Foods, 365	1/2 cup	1.30
Beans, Garbanzo or Chickpeas, Albertson's, canned	1/2 cup	3.94
Lentils, Brown, dried, boiled	1/2 cup	4.46
Lentils, Green, cooked	1/2 cup	3.86
Peas, Frozen sweet green peas, Birds Eye, boiled 5 min	2/3 cup	3.30
Peas, Green Peas, canned	1/2 cup	5.00
Peas, Split Peas, green, boiled	1/2 cup	3.72

Dairy (Most dairy has negligible amount of oxalates)

Ice Cream Bar, Original, Klondike	1 bar	8.87
Breyer's Homemade Vanilla Ice Cream	1/2 cup	1.06
Ice Cream, Haagen Dazs Butter Pecan	1/2 cup	8.98
Cheese, Mozzarella Sticks, Organic Valley	1 oz	0.17
Mozzarella, Organic, Chapel Hill Creamery, shredded	1/2 cup	2.34
Cheese, Parmesan, Kraft	1 oz	1.23
Cheese, Pepper Jack,		

Food Group	Serving size	Oxalate Value
Cache Valley Cheese, Romano,	1 oz (1/4 cup)	0.28
BelGiosio	1 oz (1/4 cup)	0.00
Cheese, Swiss, Albertson's	1 oz	1.20
Cottage Cheese, Small Curd, Organic Valley	1/2 cup	2.86
Half and Half, Horizon Organic	2 tbsp	0.00
Velveeta, Kraft	1 oz	1.09

Condiments

Red Hot Sauce, Frank's original	1 tsp	0.28
Tabasco	1 tsp	0.52
Ketchup, brand unspecified	1 tbsp	1.16
Condiment, Mayonnaise, Heinz	1 tbsp	1.68
Condiment, Mayonnaise, Hellman's	1 tbsp	0.00
Condiment, Mustard, Dijon	1 tbsp	0.99
Condiment, Mustard, Dijon	1 tsp	0.33
Mustard, Yellow, French's	1 tsp	0.30
Salsa, Picante Sauce	2 tbsp	4.50
Vinegar, Balsamic	1 tbsp	0.40
Worcestershire Sauce, French's	1 tsp	0.36

Herbs and Spices

Chives, fresh, chopped	1 tbsp	0.22
Cilantro, fresh, chopped	1/4 cup	0.94
Basil, dried	1 tsp	0.96
Cilantro Flakes, Simply Organic	1 tbsp	1.56
Dill, fresh, Organics	1 tbsp	0.70
Garlic Powder, McCormick	1 tsp	0.20
Minced Onion, dried	1 tsp	0.69
Parsley, fresh, chopped	1 tsp	1.00
Rosemary, fresh, Melissa's	1 tsp	0.36
Sage, dried, ground, McCormick	1 tsp	4.30
Ginger, ground, McCormick	1 tsp	0.68
Mustard, brand unspecified	1 tsp	0.18
Pepper, White, McCormick	1 tsp	0.68
Red Pepper, crushed, McCormick	1 tsp	1.73

Meats and Seafood (Most meats and seafood have negligible amounts)

Beef Hot Dog, uncured, Applegate Organics	1 hot dog	1.68
Chicken Breast, roasted, Sliced, Applegate Organics	2 oz	2.80
Turkey, breast, oven roasted, Oscar Meyer	3 slices	4.03
Roasted Turkey Breast, Applegate Organics	2 oz	2.13
Anchovies, King Oscar	6 fillets	0.41
Sardines, canned, King Oscar	2 Sardines	0.24
Tuna, Chunk light, Star-Kist	2 oz	7.50

***

BREADS, CRACKERS AND SNACKS

COCONUT LOAF BREAD

When you want bread by the slice without gluten or grain you'll find this bread a perfect alternative to high oxalate breads.

Serves 8
Oxalate Content Per Serving: 0.50 mg

INGREDIENTS
6 eggs, room temperature
¼ cup butter or coconut oil, melted
½ cup milk
¾ cup coconut flour
½ tsp. salt
1 ½ tsp. baking powder

1. Preheat oven to 350 degrees.
2. Mix wet ingredients in a medium bowl and whisk dry ingredients together.
3. Combine the wet and dry ingredients then pour into an oiled or silicon loaf pan.
4. Bake 40 minutes.
5. Cool for at least an hour before slicing.

COOK'S NOTE
Refrigerate up to 5 days.

CHEESE BISCUITS

A light garlic and cheddar biscuit.

Serves 4
Oxalate Content Per Serving: 0.70 mg

INGREDIENTS
5 eggs,
1 cup cheddar cheese, shredded
½ cup coconut flour
½ tsp. baking powder
¼ tsp. garlic powder
½ tsp. salt
¼ cup butter, melted
¼ cup water

1. Preheat oven to 400 degrees.
2. In a mixing bowl, beat the eggs then add the shredded cheese.
3. In a second mixing bowl, combine the flour, baking powder, garlic powder and salt.
4. Pour the egg and cheese over the flour, then add the melted butter and water.
5. Mix well and set aside for 2 minutes.
6. Drop by large spoonfuls onto parchment lined baking sheet.
7. Bake for 15 minutes and set aside to cool.

COOK'S NOTE
This recipe makes 12 great tasting low carb biscuits. These savory biscuits are grain-free, gluten-free and sugar-free.

BISCUITS

These coconut flour biscuits are gluten-free, paleo-friendly, low carb, keto and delicious!

Serves 4
Oxalate Content Per Serving: 1.83 mg

INGREDIENTS
6 eggs
¼ cup butter, melted
½ cup milk
¾ cup coconut flour
1 ½ tsp. baking powder
¼ tsp. salt

1. Preheat oven to 350 degrees.
2. Mix all ingredients and drop on a parchment lined baking sheet (makes 8).
3. Bake for 35 minutes.

COOK'S NOTE
Coconut flour will never taste like regular flour. It's basically impossible to replicate buttermilk biscuits using grain-free flours but they are buttery and a perfect replacement for high oxalate wheat flour biscuits.

COCONUT FLOUR ROUNDS

A delicious low carb, gluten-free sandwich bread that is baked flat and round rather than in a loaf.

Serves 1
Oxalate Content Per Serving: 0.10 mg

INGREDIENTS
1 ½ tbsp. coconut flour
⅛ tsp. salt
¼ tsp. baking powder
1 egg, beaten
1 tbsp. coconut oil or butter, melted

1. Preheat oven to 350 degrees.
2. Mix coconut flour, salt, and baking powder together until combined.
3. Add egg and melted coconut oil or butter and mix well.
4. Let batter sit for a few minutes to allow the flour to absorb the liquid.
5. Scoop half the batter onto a baking pan and use a spatula to spread batter into a circle the size of a bun. Repeat using the rest of the batter.
6. Bake for 10 minutes or until golden brown.

COOK'S NOTE
Coconut flour is made from dried coconut solids ground into a very fine powder. This a completely gluten-free flour. Yet unlike a lot of gluten-free flours, it is oxalate free. It's probably the easiest flour to start with if you're new to gluten-free cooking.

SOFT DINNER ROLLS

A soft and savory grain-free faux bread roll with a light texture and taste.

Serves 6
Oxalate Content Per Serving: 0 mg

INGREDIENTS
3 eggs, whites and yolks separated
⅛ tsp. cream of tartar
½ tsp. honey
⅛ tsp. salt
3 oz. cream cheese

1. Heat oven to 300 degrees.
2. In a medium-size bowl, add the egg whites and cream of tartar.
3. Using an electric mixer on high, whip the egg whites until very stiff and set aside.
4. In another medium-size bowl, add the egg yolks, honey, salt, and cream cheese.
5. Using an electric mixer on high, blend until smooth.
6. Fold the egg white mixture into the yolk mixture with a spatula.
7. Spoon 6 mounds onto an oiled baking sheet.
8. Bake 25-30 minutes.
9. Cool before removing to a serving dish.

COOK'S NOTE
This light, grain-free roll is so versatile. Serve it alongside any meal, or top it with anything from avocado to your favorite jam.

CARNIVORE CRACKERS

Quick and easy homemade crackers with healthy low oxalate natural ingredients

Serves 2
Oxalate Content Per Serving: 2.46 mg

INGREDIENTS
½ cup chicken, cooked and shredded
½ cup Parmesan cheese
1 egg

1. Preheat oven to 425 degrees.
2. Mix all ingredients and spread thin on a parchment lined baking sheet. I squared mine up to cut equal size.
3. Bake for 35 minutes.
4. Cut and cool.

COOK'S NOTE
After searching the cracker aisle looking for a grain-free cracker and realizing even the rice crackers had unhealthy ingredients. I found this homemade cracker to be the easiest and tastiest cracker to be made. To make it even easier replace ½ cup chicken with 4.5 oz canned chicken, drained.

CHEDDAR CRISPS

Crunchy cheese thins packed with flavor.

Serves 6
Oxalate Content Per Serving: 0.29 mg

INGREDIENTS
1 cup sharp cheddar cheese, shredded
⅛ tsp. salt
⅛ tsp. white pepper
¼ tsp. onion powder
¼ tsp. garlic powder

1. Preheat oven to 425 degrees and line a large baking sheet with parchment paper. (Oil the baking sheet first so that the parchment paper lies flat.)
2. Drop large spoonfuls of cheese onto the sheet leaving about an inch of space between them. Flatten them out.
3. Mix the seasoning in a small bowl and sprinkle over each of the mounds.
4. Bake for about 7 minutes until they melt completely but have not changed color.
5. Allow to cool before transferring to a serving dish.

COOK'S NOTE
Going gluten-free doesn't have to mean cracker-free. These simple cheese crisps make a light crunchy snack or a great garnish for any dish.

APPLE BARS

High protein, gluten-free, low oxalate and very filling snack that's lightly sweetened with apples and maple syrup.

Serves 12
Oxalate Content Per Serving: 4.90 mg

INGREDIENTS
½ cup coconut flour
½ tsp. baking soda
¼ tsp. salt
½ cup maple syrup
5 eggs
4 tbsp. butter, melted
1 small red apple, chopped (use one for the batter and one for the topping)

1. Preheat oven to 400 degrees.
2. In a large bowl combine all ingredients except the apple and mix well on low speed.
4. Stir in 1 cup apple and pour into a 9×12 baking dish.
5. Bake for 30 minutes. Cool before topping.

TOPPING
1 small red apple, chopped
¼ cup raw sugar
1 cup sour cream

1. Cook the apples and sugar until soft and set aside to cool while the cake bakes.
2. Let the cake and apples cool.
3. Finish the topping by beating the sour cream until you have stiff peaks and then fold in the apple mix.
4. Top, cut and serve.

COOK'S NOTE
The size of your baking dish will determine the height of the bars. I like to use 8×8 silicone bake-ware but a 9×12 casserole dish is fine.

CORNSTARCH AND EGG WRAPS

Just 2 ingredient no flour wrap for burritos, egg rolls or sandwich wraps.

Serves 1
Oxalate Content Per Serving: 0 mg

INGREDIENTS
1 egg white
¼ tsp. cornstarch
¼ tsp. water

1. Whisk together until smooth.
2. Pour into a lightly oiled non stick skillet and fry over medium heat until golden brown.

COOK'S NOTE
These are so easy to make when you can't seem to find a wrap that doesn't have flour or cornmeal in the ingredients.

BUFFALO CHICKEN CHEDDAR BITES

A quick and easy spicy snack.

Serves 6
Oxalate Content Per Serving: 1.70 mg

INGREDIENTS
1 ¼ cup chicken, cooked and shredded
1 cup cheddar cheese, shredded
Tabasco sauce

1. Preheat oven to 400 degrees.
2. In a 12 cup muffin tin, add in a thin layer of cheese, a layer of chicken with a sprinkle of Tabasco sauce in and top with another layer of cheese in each cup.
3. Bake for 5-6 minutes.
4. Remove to a paper towel until cooled a bit and serve.

COOK'S NOTE
An alternative is to replace ½ cup chicken with 4.5 oz canned chicken, drained.

NO CORNMEAL CORNBREAD

Coconut flour, Greek yogurt and fresh corn come together to make this low oxalate cornbread that's full of flavor and will satisfy that desire for traditional cornbread.

Serves 8
Oxalate Content Per Serving: 0.67 mg

INGREDIENTS
6 tbsp. coconut flour
1 tsp. baking powder
½ tsp. baking soda
¼ tsp. salt
½ cup plain whole milk yogurt
3 tbsp. butter, melted
3 eggs
1 ½ cup corn

1. Preheat oven to 400 degrees.
2. Mix dry ingredients in a medium sized bowl.
3. Puree corn in a blender.
4. Combine all wet ingredients in a medium sized bowl and mix at low speed until smooth.
5. Add in the dry ingredients and mix well.
6. Pour into an oiled baking dish and bake for 40 minutes.

COOK'S NOTE
This recipe was born out of my desire to enjoy the old fashioned chicken and dressing my grandmother used to make every Thanksgiving. Just a little change in her recipe brought it back to my table.

CHICKEN AND CHEESE PIZZA CRUST

This chicken and cheese crust bakes into a wonderfully sturdy and tasty crust that will hold up to any topping.

Serves 2
Oxalate Content Per Serving: 0 mg

INGREDIENTS
1 ¼ cup chicken, cooked and shredded
1 cup cheddar, shredded
1 large egg
½ tsp. garlic

1. Preheat oven to 400 degrees.
2. Mix well in a medium sized bowl.
3. Spread thin on a parchment lined baking sheet.
4. Bake for 20 minutes.

COOK'S NOTE
This recipe is simple and creates a crispy crust for pizza or flatbread, but it also can be pressed a little thinner in rounds for sandwich bread or buns for hot dogs. To make it even easier replace chicken with 10 oz canned chicken, drained.

TOASTED COCONUT CHIPS

Save big when you make these toasted coconut chips yourself. Salt them and you'll be happy to replace your high oxalate potato chips for these fresh baked chips.

Serves 6
Oxalate Content Per Serving: 0 mg

INGREDIENTS
2 cups unsweetened coconut chips
1 tsp. salt

1. Preheat oven to 350 degrees.
2. Spread the coconut chips on a parchment lined baking sheet.
3. Bake for 5-6 minutes.
4. Salt the chips and allow them to cool before storing in a plastic bag.

COOK'S NOTE
Replacing potato chips was a daunting task until I realized toasted coconut had that crunch I missed and salting them created a snack equal to the high oxalate potato chips I had to give up.

***

BREAKFAST DISHES

CREAM OF COCONUT

A delicious hot cereal very similar to cream of wheat.

Serves 1
Oxalate Content Per Serving: 1.56 mg

INGREDIENTS
2 tbsp. coconut flour
¾ cup water
2 tsp. butter
2 tsp. honey
¼ tsp. salt
1 egg, beaten

1. Bring all ingredients except the egg to a simmer on medium heat.
2. Lower the heat and whisk in the egg for 30 seconds.
3. Remove from heat and serve.

COOK'S NOTE
It may taste much like cream of wheat, but this recipe is gluten-free and high in protein.

CLOUD BREAD CHEESE DANISH

These homemade danishes are lightly sweetened and are so creamy and soft.

Serves 8
Oxalate Content Per Serving: 0.41 mg

INGREDIENTS
2 tbsp. cream cheese, softened
2 large eggs, whites and yolks separated
½ tsp. honey
¼ tsp. salt
¼ tsp. cream of tartar

FILLING
5 oz. cream cheese, softened
¼ tsp. vanilla
2 tbsp. honey
Juice of ½ lemon
1 tbsp. butter, melted

1. Preheat oven to 300 degrees.
2. In a medium size bowl mix cream cheese, egg yolks, honey and salt at low speed.
3. In a separate bowl beat the egg whites and cream of tarter until stiff.
4. Carefully and quickly fold them together and place large spoonfuls on a parchment lined baking sheet.
5. Bake for 20 minutes.
6. Make the filling by mixing all ingredients together.
7. Place a spoonful of filling into the middle of each danish.
8. Allow to cool before serving.

COOK'S NOTE
It's impossible to locate a Danish pastry on the market made without grain flour and unnatural ingredients. These homemade danish pastries turn out tastier than anything you can find on the shelves.

SOS

Ground beef and gravy was a military dish my dad served when I was young. It was served over toast but serving it over eggs instead makes it gluten-free and low oxalate.

Serves 8
Oxalate Content Per Serving: 0 mg

INGREDIENTS
1 lb. ground beef
1 tsp. cornstarch
1 cup milk

1. Stir fry ground beef until done.
2. Mix cornstarch, milk, and a spoonful of meat together in a small bowl until smooth.
3. Add another spoonful of the meat, stir and pour slowly into the skillet.
4. Bring to a simmer and remove from heat.
5. Serve over scrambled eggs.

COOK'S NOTE
Using low oxalate cornstarch is the easiest way to make gravy in any recipe.

SAUSAGE

A simple recipe for making your own classic, tasty sausage patties.

Serves 6 (Makes 12 patties.)
Oxalate Content Per Serving: 0.47 mg

INGREDIENTS
1 lb. ground pork, grass fed-beef, bison or venison
1 tbsp. white wine vinegar
1 tsp. onion, diced
1 tsp. Dijon mustard
½ tsp. sage
½ tsp. rosemary
¼ tsp. salt
½ tsp. white pepper
½ tsp. garlic powder
2 tbsp. coconut oil (for frying)

1. In a large mixing bowl, combine all of the ingredients and mix well.
2. Form patties and cook in an oiled nonstick skillet over medium-high heat until golden brown on both sides.
3. Serve hot.

COOK'S NOTE
Say goodbye to all those food additives and make your own sausage. You'll never go back to buying ready-made again.

BUTTERY BANANA MUFFINS

A moist and wholesome muffin with all natural ingredients.

Serves 6
Oxalate Content Per Serving: 0.10 mg

INGREDIENTS
½ cup coconut flour
½ tsp. baking powder
1 tsp. baking soda
½ tsp. salt
5 eggs
1 cup banana, very ripe and mashed
½ tsp. vanilla
2 tbsp. maple syrup
¼ cup butter, melted

1. Preheat oven to 400 degrees and oil a 12 cup muffin pan or line with paper cupcake liners.
2. In a large bowl, mix the coconut flour, baking powder, baking soda and salt.
3. In a separate bowl, combine the eggs, mashed banana, vanilla, maple syrup and melted butter. Whisk well.
4. Pour the egg mix over the coconut flour and mix well.
5. Fill muffin cups two-thirds to three-quarters full.
6. Bake for 14-15 minutes. Remove when they start to brown and a toothpick inserted in the center comes out clean.
7. Allow to cool for about 5 minutes before transferring to serving dish.
8. Serve warm with a pat of butter on top.

COOK'S NOTE
Use very ripe bananas for a more intense banana flavor.

HAM AND CHEESE EGG PUFFS

Easy, baked, high protein savory biscuits that are not only for breakfast, but can be packed in lunchboxes or for an on the go snack.

Serves 4
Oxalate Content Per Serving: 0.50 mg

INGREDIENTS
2 eggs
3 tbsp. coconut flour
½ cup ham, chopped
¼ cup onion, diced
1 cup cheddar, shredded
¼ tsp. garlic powder
¼ tsp. white pepper

1. Preheat oven to 350 degrees.
2. Combine all ingredients and mix well.
3. Form small 1 ½ inch rounds and press them down a little on a parchment lined baking sheet.
4. Bake for 30 minutes.

COOK'S NOTE
Pork is rich in selenium, zinc, phosphorus, potassium and iron and may make a useful inclusion for supporting thyroid function, immunity, bone health and energy production.

YOGURT PANCAKES

Easy, delicious, grain-free and protein rich pancakes.

Serves 2
Oxalate Content Per Serving: 3.53 mg

INGREDIENTS
½ cup coconut flour
¼ tsp. baking soda
¼ tsp. salt
4 eggs, beaten
1 tbsp. butter, melted
½ tsp. vanilla
½ cup plain whole milk yogurt
3 tbsp. water
Coconut oil (for frying)
¼ cup maple syrup

1. In a medium-size bowl, mix the coconut flour, baking soda and salt together.
2. In a separate bowl, beat the eggs; then add the butter and vanilla, yogurt and water.
3. Pour the egg mixture over the coconut flour and mix well. Allow the mix to sit a minute or two to thicken.
4. In a large nonstick skillet, heat a small amount of coconut oil over medium heat.
5. Pour palm size cakes and shake the skillet a bit to spread them out without touching each other. (In a large skillet you can cook 2 or 3 at a time.)
6. Cook for about 2-3 minutes, until bubbly on top, and then turn. Cook an additional 2 minutes or until golden brown.
7. Serve hot with maple syrup.

SAUSAGE AND EGG MUFFINS

A high protein grab and go complete breakfast when they are made ahead of time.

Serves 6
Oxalate Content Per Serving: 0.81mg

INGREDIENTS
¼ cup butter, melted
¼ cup milk
6 eggs, beaten
½ cup coconut flour
1 tsp. baking soda
¼ tsp. salt
½ cup cheddar, shredded
8 oz. crumbled sausage

1. Preheat oven to 350 degrees.
2. Mix wet ingredients in a medium sized bowl.
3. Whisk the coconut flour, baking soda and salt together and add the wet. Mix well.
4. Add in the sausage and the cheese. Mix well.
5. Fill 12 muffin cups and bake for 30 minutes.
6. Serve warm.

COOK'S NOTE
Eggs are the powerhouse of nutrition.

***

SOUPS, SALADS AND DRESSINGS

SLOW COOKER CHICKEN STEW

This flavorful stew features chicken breasts along with low oxalate vegetables and just a bit of sour cream for added fat.

Serves 4
Oxalate Content Per Serving: 4.39 mg

INGREDIENTS
2 large chicken breasts
1 medium yellow onion, chopped
½ red bell pepper, chopped
3 cups water
¼ tsp. garlic powder
¼ tsp. salt
1 cup cauliflower, chopped
½ cup green peas
½ corn
¼ cup sour cream

1. Add the chicken, onion, bell pepper, water, garlic and salt to the slow cooker and set on high for 4-6 hours.
2. Shred the chicken and add in the remaining ingredients.
3. Cook for another 30 minutes and serve hot.

VEGETABLE SOUP

A cozy bowl of comforting soup filled with an array of colorful veggies, with low oxalate vegetables and a pinch of seasoning

Serves 4
Oxalate Content Per Serving: 4.35 mg

INGREDIENTS
1 medium yellow onion, chopped
2 garlic cloves, minced
1 red bell pepper, chopped
2 tbsp. coconut oil
3 cups water
1 medium bok choy, chopped
2 cups cauliflower, chopped
1 cup corn
½ tsp. salt
½ tsp. white pepper
½ tsp. garlic powder
1 tsp. fresh rosemary

1. In a large saucepan stir-fry the onion, garlic and bell pepper in the coconut oil.
2. Add in the remaining ingredients and bring to a boil.
3. Reduce heat to simmer for about 20 minutes.

COOK'S NOTE
Bok choy is an excellent source of vitamins A and C, which are antioxidants that can help protect the immune system and repair cell damage. It also contains vitamins B6, K, and E, magnesium, potassium, iron, manganese and calcium.

CORN CHOWDER

This thick and easy, delicious recipe is the perfect comfort food full of flavors so bold you'll want to eat this soup often.

Serves 4
Oxalate Content Per Serving: 2.05 mg

INGREDIENTS
1 yellow onion, chopped
1 red bell pepper, chopped
2 garlic cloves, minced
4 tbsp. butter or ghee
1 bag (16 oz.) frozen sweet corn
¼ cup olive oil
2 cups water
2 cups bone or chicken broth
½ cup plain whole milk yogurt or heavy whipping cream
¼ cup cream cheese
¼ tsp. salt
4 oz. cheddar cheese, shredded

1. In a large skillet, stir fry the onion, bell pepper and garlic in the butter until soft. Add the frozen sweet corn and the olive oil and cook for about 3 minutes.
2. Pour the mix into a blender, add water and blend until smooth but with some corn kernels whole.
3. Pour the blended corn into a soup pot and add remaining ingredients.
4. Bring to a boil, and then reduce the heat to medium and simmer for about 10 minutes.
5. Add salt and cheddar cheese.

COOK'S NOTE
Corn can support the growth of friendly bacteria..

SPLIT PEA SOUP

A deliciously simple yet hearty split pea soup made from a short list of ingredients.

Serves 6
Oxalate Content Per Serving: 6.02 mg

INGREDIENTS
1 tbsp. butter
1 yellow onion, chopped
½ tsp. salt
2 cups dried split green peas, picked over and rinsed
5 cups water

1. Add butter to a big pot over med-high heat.
2. Stir in onions and salt and cook until the onions soften, just a minute or two.
3. Add the split peas and water. Bring to a boil then turn down the heat.
Simmer for 20 minutes, or until the peas are cooked through but still a touch al dente.
4. Pour half of the cooked peas into a blender and puree smooth.
6. Return it to the pot, and it's ready to serve.

COOK'S NOTE
Split peas are dried, peeled and split in half sweet green peas. Split peas are a great source of protein and fiber. They are also rich in minerals such as magnesium, potassium and zinc.

ARUGULA AND CAULIFLOWER SOUP

Cauliflower combined with arugula makes a delicious, thick peppery soup.

Serves 6
Oxalate Content Per Serving: 2.23 mg

INGREDIENTS
2 tbsp. butter
1 yellow onion, chopped
2 garlic cloves, chopped
1 large head cauliflower, chopped
3 cups water
2 cups milk
2 cups arugula leaves
½ tsp. salt
½ tsp. white pepper

1. Heat the butter in a large soup pot then add the onion and garlic. Cook for about 6-8 minutes over medium heat to lightly color and soften the onion.
2. Add the roughly chopped cauliflower and water to the pan. Bring to a boil, then reduce the heat to low and simmer for 15–20 minutes.
3. Add the milk and arugula and warm without letting the soup boil.
4. Add the salt and pepper.
5. Process half the soup in a blender.
6. Return it to the soup pot, stir and serve.

COOK'S NOTE
Arugula is a low-calorie and low oxalate food. A full cup of arugula contains just five calories and is high in calcium and iron.

CLAM CHOWDER

A delicious and warming creamy clam chowder that has a perfectly mild, briny flavor and creamy texture with a touch of bacon for a rich, smoky flavor.

Serves 4
Oxalate Content Per Serving: 1.46 mg

INGREDIENTS
4 slices bacon, cooked and chopped
½ small yellow onion, diced
¼ tsp. white pepper
2 (10 oz.) cans whole baby clams with juice
1 tbsp. corn starch
½ cup white wine
Juice of ½ lemon
½ cup heavy cream or whole milk
1 cup white Jasmine rice, cooked

1. In a large skillet, fry the bacon and set the bacon aside.
2 Saute onions in the bacon fat.
3. Add the remaining ingredients and simmer on low for 15 minutes.
4. Top with bacon and serve.

COOK'S NOTE
Clams are one of the most nutritious foods in the world, and they offer an exceptional range of nutrients. They are one of the best dietary sources of vitamin B12. Following vitamin B12, the second most concentrated micro-nutrient in clams is iron.

CHICKEN NOODLE SOUP

Making chicken noodle soup from scratch is a step above the rest, made with white rice pasta and homemade chicken broth.

Serves 4
Oxalate Content Per Serving: 1.50 mg

INGREDIENTS
4 tbsp. butter
4 boneless chicken thighs
1 tsp. garlic powder
½ tsp. salt
¼ tsp. white pepper
½ onion, diced
8 oz dry white rice pasta, (I use Simple Truth Organic Pad Thai white rice pasta.)
1 cup chicken broth

1. Melt butter in a large skillet over medium high heat and pan sear the chicken for about 5 minutes on each side.
2. Slice into small pieces and add the seasonings and onion.
3. Continue to cook the chicken and onions stirring occasionally for about 5 minutes.
4. Prepare pasta using packaged directions and drain.
5. Add in 2 cups of water and scrape the bits from the bottom of the skillet.
6. Add both the drained pasta and the chicken to a large pot along with another cup of chicken broth.
7. Bring to a boil and remove from heat.

EGG DROP SOUP

This simple and tasty egg drop soup tastes just like the soup at your favorite Chinese restaurant.

Serves 6
Oxalate Content Per Serving: 0 mg

INGREDIENTS
4 cups chicken broth
1 tsp. coconut oil
½ tsp. salt
¼ tsp. white pepper
3 tbsp. cornstarch
1/3 cup water
3 eggs, beaten
¼ tsp. chives

1. Bring the chicken broth to a simmer in a medium soup pot and stir in the coconut oil, salt and pepper.
2. In a separate bowl, add the cornstarch and 1/3 cup water along with another 1/3 cup warmed broth and mix until smooth.
3. Stir the soup continuously as you drizzle in the cornstarch mix or you'll get clumps of cooked starch in your soup. Use a ladle to stir the soup in a circular motion, and slowly drizzle in the egg until you have added it all.
6. Pour soup into bowls, top with chives, and serve.

COOK'S NOTE
In one bowl of egg drop soup, you get 370 milligrams of potassium and trace amounts of calcium, folate, iron, vitamin B-12, vitamin C, vitamin D and zinc.

VEGETABLE PASTA SALAD

An easy, cold and colorful vegetable pasta salad.

Serves 4
Oxalate Content Per Serving: 5.00 mg

INGREDIENTS
8 oz dry white rice pasta, (I use Simple Truth Organic Pad Thai white rice pasta.)

DRESSING
6 tbsp. plain whole milk yogurt or sour cream
¼ cup butter, melted
1 garlic clove, finely minced
2 tbsp. yellow onion, diced
¼ tsp. salt
¼ tsp. pepper

SALAD VEGETABLES
1 cup baby arugula, chopped
1 cup frozen peas
1 cup frozen corn

1. Cook the pasta using packaged directions.
2. Prepare the dressing by whisking together the yogurt, butter, garlic, onion, salt and pepper in a bowl.
3. One minute before the pasta is finished cooking to al dente, add the arugula, peas, and corn to the water.
4. Drain the pasta and vegetables in a large colander and rinse with cold water until completely cooled. If it's still hot, it will absorb too much of the dressing.
5. Add the drained and cooled pasta and vegetables to a large bowl and toss with the dressing.

WARM HAM AND EGG SALAD

Perfect high protein warm salad for a cold day

Serves 1
Oxalate Content Per Serving: 2.52 mg

INGREDIENTS
½ cup romaine, chopped
½ cup arugula, chopped
2 thin slices of yellow onion
3 thin slices of red bell pepper
2 tbsp. butter
3 slices ham
1 tbsp. Dijon mustard
1 egg

1. Add the romaine and arugula to a salad plate.
2. Stir fry thinly sliced onion and red pepper in butter until soft and stir in the ham. Heat and place on the lettuce on the salad plate.
3. Top with Dijon mustard and mix these ingredients.
4. Cook an egg to your preference and add atop the salad.

COOK'S NOTE
You find this salad called Salade Lyonnaise, served as an appetizer across France.

CHICKEN CAESAR SALAD

Transform the classic Caesar into a main-course salad by topping it with seared chicken breasts, Parmesan, and a fresh, bold, easy homemade Caesar dressing.

Serves 2
Oxalate Content Per Serving: 1.63 mg

INGREDIENTS
2 tbsp. coconut oil, or ghee
2 boneless chicken breasts
2 cups romaine lettuce, chopped
2 oz Parmesan cheese (as topping)

1. In a non-stick frying pan, heat oil over medium-high heat and place the chicken in the hot oil. Cook for 4 minutes on each side.
2. Check if it's cooked by poking the tip of a sharp knife into the thickest part; there should be no sign of pink and juices will run clear. Set aside.
3. Divide the romaine lettuce into 2 large bowls.
4. Place sliced chicken breasts on top of lettuce, top with Caesar dressing (next page) and garnish with Parmesan.

COOK'S NOTE
Each ingredient of a chicken Caesar salad contains beneficial properties for your health. By making your own you have the ability to get rid of a ton of chemicals, additives, and other artificial ingredients. If you look at the ingredient list of most bottled salad dressings, you'll notice soybean, canola, or some other kind of vegetable oil is listed as one of the first ingredients. Cheap and easy to manufacture, refined oils are actually pretty bad for your health.

CAESAR DRESSING

Serves 2
Oxalate Content Per Serving: 2.35 mg

INGREDIENTS
3 garlic cloves
¼ cup olive oil
¼ tsp. Worcestershire sauce
2 tbsp. white wine vinegar
1 egg
1 tsp. dry mustard
¼ cup Parmesan, grated
¼ tsp. white pepper
4 anchovies

1. Add all of the ingredients to a blender and process for 30 seconds until the mixture is smooth.
2. Shake or whisk well before serving.

COOK'S NOTE
Once you've tried this Caesar dressing recipe you will never buy bottled Caesar dressing again.

HONEY MUSTARD DRESSING

Serves 4
Oxalate Content Per Serving: 3.19 mg

INGREDIENTS
½ cup mustard
¼ cup honey
¼ cup plain whole milk yogurt
1 tbsp. olive oil
1 tbsp. white wine vinegar

1. Place all of the ingredients in a jar, cover tightly, and shake.
2. Shake or whisk well before serving.

ITALIAN DRESSING

Serves 4
Oxalate Content Per Serving: 1.29 mg

INGREDIENTS
½ cup olive oil
¼ cup white wine vinegar
¼ tsp. garlic powder
¼ tsp. dried rosemary
¼ tsp. dried oregano
¼ tsp. dried basil

1. Place all of the ingredients in a jar, cover tightly, and shake.
2. Allow to sit at least 30 minutes to meld the ingredients.
3. Shake or whisk well before serving.

RANCH DRESSING

Serves 4
Oxalate Content Per Serving: 0.21 mg

INGREDIENTS
½ cup butter
½ tsp., garlic powder
½ tsp. chives
¼ tsp. onion powder
¼ tsp. fresh parsley
¼ tsp. dried dill
1 cup plain whole milk yogurt

1. Melt the butter, whisk in all of the seasonings, and mix in the yogurt.
2. Allow to sit at least 20 minutes to meld the ingredients.
3. Bring to room temperature and shake well before serving.

***

MAIN DISHES

GROUND BEEF STIR-FRY

This quick and easy stir-fry dinner is delicious on its own, but I often serve it over white rice for a heartier meal.

Serves 4
Oxalate Content Per Serving: 6.66 mg

INGREDIENTS
1 lb. ground grass-fed beef
1 large yellow onion, chopped
½ red bell pepper, thinly sliced
½ tsp. salt
½ tsp. garlic powder
4 cups Savoy cabbage, chopped
1 cup white Jasmine rice, cooked (optional) (add 4.37 mg oxalate)

1. Brown beef in a large skillet or wok.
2. When the beef is almost completely browned add the onion, red pepper, salt and garlic.
3. When the onions have started to soften, add the cabbage. (Add a small amount of water to steam the cabbage if it starts to stick to the skillet.)
4. Cook for about 2-3 minutes more, stirring often until the cabbage softens.
5. Serve as main dish or over rice.

BEEF CASSEROLE

One dish hearty dinner that is quite forgiving when it comes to substitutions, especially the rice instead of high oxalate potatoes.

Serves 6
Oxalate Content Per Serving: 1.50 mg

INGREDIENTS
1 pound ground beef
1 tsp. garlic powder
½ tsp. white pepper
1 tbsp. butter or ghee (for frying onion)
½ large yellow onion, chopped
1 cup white Jasmine rice, cooked
1 cup cheddar, shredded
4 eggs

1. Preheat oven to 400 degrees.
2. Stir-fry beef and season with garlic and pepper. Remove it to a dish to cool.
3. Cook the onion in butter until soft.
4. Layer in a casserole dish, the cooked beef mixed with one egg, the cooked onion mixed with one egg, the cooked rice mixed with one egg and top with cheddar and 1 egg.
5. Bake for 15 minutes and then place under broiler for an additional 5-6 minutes to brown the cheese top.

COOK'S NOTE
Protein is essential for healthy muscle growth, as well as being the most important nutrient in your blood. Secondly, rice is a good source of energy. It contains complex carbs that are excellent in fulfilling energy needs.

UNSTUFFED BELL PEPPER BOWL

This recipe can be ready in 20 minutes which definitely beats the traditional preparation and time of regular stuffed peppers.

Serves 4
Oxalate Content Per Serving: 1.80 mg

INGREDIENTS
½ medium yellow onion, sliced
½ red bell pepper, sliced
4 tbsp. butter
1 lb ground beef
¼ tsp. salt
½ tsp. garlic powder
1 cup white Jasmine rice, cooked
1 cup American cheese

1. Stir fry the onion and bell pepper in butter until soft. Remove and set aside.
2. Cook the ground beef and season with salt and garlic powder.
3. Melt the cheese.
4. In 2 bowls add the rice, ground beef, onion and peppers, and top with cheese.

COOK'S NOTE
Bell peppers are low in calories and rich in vitamin C and other antioxidants, making them an excellent addition to a healthy diet.

SALMON SCRAMBLE

A classic combination of creamy scrambled eggs and chunks of buttery salmon.

Serves 4
Oxalate Content Per Serving: 0 mg

INGREDIENTS
5 eggs
1 tbsp. whole milk
¼ tsp. salt
⅛ tsp. white pepper
1 tbsp. fresh chopped chives
2 tbsp. butter or ghee
1 can (14 oz.) wild Alaskan salmon, drained

1. In a medium-size mixing bowl, combine the egg, milk, salt, pepper and chives. Blend well.
2. In a large nonstick skillet, heat the butter over medium heat and pour in the egg mixture.
3. Stir eggs until almost set then gently stir in and break up the salmon.
4. Continue to cook until salmon is warmed and the eggs are set.
5. Serve hot.

COOK'S NOTE
This quick and easy low-carbohydrate, protein and omega-3 rich breakfast will satisfy the heartiest appetite. Each serving supplies 64% of your daily requirement for vitamin B12 and 44% of your daily requirement for vitamin B6.

PORK CHOPS IN WINE AND GARLIC SAUCE

These tender and delicious pork chops with wine and garlic sauce are a new favorite, easy dinner recipe around here. One skillet, little mess.

Serves 2
Oxalate Content Per Serving: 0.39 mg

INGREDIENTS
4 tbsp. butter or ghee
3 tbsp. garlic, minced
4 small pork chops
¼ cup cornstarch
1 cup red wine
½ cup water
1 tbsp. balsamic vinegar

1. Heat the butter and garlic in a skillet to infuse.
2. Lightly dredge the pork chops in the cornstarch.
3. Add the pork chops and sear 2 minutes each side.
3. Remove the pork chops and set aside.
4. Reduce the heat to medium/high and add the red wine. Stir to release the skillet bits and cook until reduced (about minutes).
5. Add in water, vinegar and the pork chops.
6. Simmer another 5-6 minutes and serve. with a side salad or over rice.

COOK'S NOTE
Pork is an excellent source of thiamin, niacin, riboflavin, vitamin B6, and phosphorus. It is a good source of zinc and potassium.

KENTUCKY-STYLE BOURBON BARBECUE ROAST

A melt in your mouth chuck roast prepared in the slow cooker and finished with a flavorful sauce that is off the charts.

Serves 8
Oxalate Content Per Serving: 1.31 mg

INGREDIENTS
3 lb beef chuck roast
1 yellow onion, chopped
3 cups water
¼ cup white wine vinegar
¼ tsp. salt
¼ tsp. garlic powder
¼ cup Bourbon
½ cup maple syrup
2 tbsp. tart cherry juice
2 tsp. white pepper

1. Place the chuck roast in a slow cooker with onion and water, vinegar, salt, and garlic powder and Bourbon. Cook on high for 6-7 hours. It should be ready to pull apart easily.
2. Add the meat with it's liquids to a large skillet and shred.
3. Add the maple syrup, cherry juice and white pepper.
4. Continue to cook until thick.

COOK'S NOTE
Adding Bourbon will not only enhance the flavors already present but will contribute some of the intense flavors that Bourbon is known for, namely smoke, a honeyed or caramel sweetness, and nuttiness.

BAKED LEMON ROSEMARY CHICKEN

Lemon and rosemary complement the richly roasted flavor of the chicken in this easy all-in-one dinner.

Serves 4
Oxalate Content Per Serving: 4.67 mg

INGREDIENTS
1 pound skinless, boneless chicken breasts, cut 2×2 inch squares
1 red bell pepper, thickly sliced
1 small zucchini, thickly sliced
1 medium yellow onion, cut in 1 inch chunks
¼ cup olive oil
Juice of 1 large lemon
3 cloves fresh garlic, diced
½ tsp. salt
½ tsp. dried rosemary

1. Preheat oven to 425 degrees.
2. In a large 16 inch roasting pan, combine all of the ingredients and toss until all ingredients are well coated.
3. Bake 25-30 minutes. Turn on the broiler for the last 2-3 minutes to slightly brown the top and serve.

COOK'S NOTE
Rosemary is a fragrant herb with needle-like leaves that's known for having a wide array of health benefits. You have a winning immune boosting combination when you pair rosemary with garlic and onions in a recipe.

SALISBURY STEAK

Salisbury steak is basically seasoned hamburger patties taken up a notch by cooking them in a luscious gravy.

Serves 4
Oxalate Content Per Serving: 1.58 mg

INGREDIENTS
1 lb. ground beef or bison
½ small yellow onion, diced
1 egg
¼ tsp. salt
¼ tsp. white pepper
2 tbsp. butter
6.5 oz. mushrooms
¼ tsp. garlic powder
1 cup milk
1 cup water
1 tbsp. corn starch

1. In a large bowl, combine the beef, onion, egg, salt and pepper. Form 4 patties.
2. Heat butter in a large skillet and cook the patties over medium-high heat until seared on both sides.
3. Remove the patties and turn the heat down to medium.
4. Add the mushrooms and garlic, stirring until warm. Then add in the milk and stir it to pick up the pieces left on the bottom of the skillet.
5. Mix the cornstarch and water together and add to the skillet. Continue to stir until the gravy thickens (about 2 minutes).
6. Add the beef patties back and baste them as they reheat.

COOK'S NOTE
Salisbury Steak got its start as a famous food in America when it was used as high-protein meals for soldiers during the American Civil War. It was a simple, nutritious taste of home and comfort food for soldiers. The classic flavor of Salisbury steak and gravy is very rich and satisfying.

PORK CHOPS IN GRAVY

These juicy pork chops are seasoned and pan fried. Then they're smothered in an easy homemade gravy and simmered until tender and juicy.

Serves 4
Oxalate Content Per Serving: 0.60 mg

INGREDIENTS
4 tbsp. butter or ghee
1 yellow onion, chopped
4 pork chops
1 cup water
1 tbsp. cornstarch
1/3 cup milk

1. Sear the pork chops in the butter on medium-high heat for 3 minutes on each side.
2. Remove and set aside.
3. Saute the onion in the butter until tender. Add the water.
4. Mix the cornstarch and milk together and gradually add to the skillet. Stir continually until thickened.
4. Add the pork chops back and simmer for about 6 minutes more.

COOK'S NOTE
Cornstarch thickens sauces in a snap.

CHICKEN MARSALA

Chicken Marsala is an Italian-American dish of golden pan-fried chicken and mushrooms in a rich Marsala wine sauce. It's a classic restaurant dish yet it's really easy to make at home.

Serves 6
Oxalate Content Per Serving: 1.11 mg

INGREDIENTS
2 chicken breasts
2 tbsp. butter
2 tbsp. coconut oil
½ yellow onion, diced
½ cup mushrooms
4 tbsp. butter
2 tsp. cornstarch
2 cups water
½ cup Marsala wine
8 oz dry white rice pasta (I use Simple Truth Organic Pad Thai white rice pasta)

1. Add butter and coconut oil to a large skillet on medium-high heat.
2. Sear chicken 3-5 minutes on each side.
3. Remove chicken and set aside.
4. Saute the onion until soft. Add butter and then add in mushrooms.
5. Cook 2-3 minutes and reduce the heat down to medium.
6. Mix the cornstarch in the water and add it to the skillet along with the wine.
7. Add the chicken back and lower the heat to keep a low simmer.

8. Cook for about 10-12 minutes occasionally basting the chicken.
9. Prepare the rice using packaged directions.
10. Add the cooked and drained pasta to the skillet.
11. Stir to coat it in sauce and serve.

COOK'S NOTE

I recommend using Marsala wine for this recipe, though a dry red or just simply leaving the wine out would work. You could substitute with more chicken broth but you won't get quite the same depth of flavor or sweetness from the chicken broth.

SEARED MAHI-MAHI SALAD

A refreshing light meal packed with flavor and nutrition. Pan-seared mahi-mahi is an easy to cook firm, delicate flavored fish.

Serves 2
Oxalate Content Per Serving: 4.79 mg

INGREDIENTS
DRESSING
1 tsp. dried basil
¼ tsp. Tabasco sauce
1 tbsp. balsamic vinaigrette
½ tsp. honey
1 tbsp. extra virgin olive oil

SALAD
8 cherry tomatoes, halved
2 cups arugula
1 large radish, sliced into thin strips

FISH
3 tbsp. cornstarch
¼ tsp. salt
¼ tsp. white pepper
2 tbsp. coconut oil
1 pkg. (12 oz.) frozen mahi-mahi fillets, thawed and patted dry. (Can substitute with grouper, snapper or sea bass)

1. Blend the dressing ingredients together and set aside.
2. Prepare the salad ingredients and divide onto 2 plates.
3. On a large plate combine cornstarch, salt and pepper.
4. Add coconut oil to a hot skillet.

5. Dredge both sides of the fish in the cornstarch, patting off excess.
6. Cook fish on one side to a light golden brown, for about 3-4 minutes, then turn and cook an additional 3 minutes lowering the heat to medium.
7. Place the fish in the center of each salad plate.
8. Drizzle the salad with dressing and serve immediately.

COOK'S NOTE
Fish is one of the healthiest foods you can eat. The good fat and protein has been shown to fight heart disease, boost brain health and improve skin and hair. However, these benefits can be canceled out if it's contaminated with antibiotics or chemicals. Avoid farmed fish by looking for the words "wild-caught" on the fish packaging.

SALMON PASTA CASSEROLE

A rich and hearty meal full of calcium and omega-3 fatty acids.

Serves 4
Oxalate Content Per Serving: 7.84

INGREDIENTS
8 oz dry white rice pasta (I use Simple Truth Organic Pad Thai white rice pasta)
1 cup broccoli florets
1 cup frozen sweet peas
1 can (14 oz.) wild-caught salmon, drained
2 eggs
1 tbsp. lemon juice
2 medium green onions, chopped
1 cup plain whole milk yogurt
1 cup cheddar cheese, shredded

1. Preheat oven to 350 degrees.
2. Cook rice noodles according to package directions along with the broccoli florets and peas.
3. Drain the pasta, peas and broccoli and set aside.
4. In a large mixing bowl, flake the salmon and mix it with the eggs and lemon juice; then stir in the green onions, yogurt and cheese.
5. Lightly oil a 9×13 casserole dish.
6. Layer the dish with the cooked pasta, peas, and broccoli and top with salmon mix.
7. Bake for 20 minutes. It will start to bubble round the edges and turn a golden color. You don't want to let it get too dark, the fish will overcook.

COOK'S NOTE
Pad Thai noodles are a great replacement for wheat pasta in this salmon pasta casserole. The texture and flavor are very similar. Canned salmon is calcium rich, provides high quality protein, and is an omega-3 powerhouse

ASIAN PORK PATTIES

One unique ingredient makes these delicious pork patties tender inside and crispy on the outside.

Serves 4
Oxalate Content Per Serving: 0.16 mg

INGREDIENTS
3 tbsp. coconut oil
1 lb ground pork
¼ yellow onion, diced
¼ tsp. garlic powder
¼ tsp. white pepper
¼ tsp. salt
1 egg
1 tsp. cornstarch

1. Mix ground pork with all of the ingredients.
2. Form patties any size but keep them thin for faster cooking.
3. Fry in coconut oil till done.

COOKS NOTE
These pair really well with spicy bok choy slaw (see page 145).

PORK SAUSAGE CASSEROLE

An easy and incredibly delicious breakfast for dinner meal.

Serves 4
Oxalate Content Per Serving: 1.28 mg

INGREDIENTS
1 lb. ground pork (grass fed-beef is another option)
1 tbsp. Dijon mustard
½ tsp. sage
½ tsp. rosemary
¼ tsp. salt
1 tsp. white pepper
½ tsp. garlic powder
½ medium yellow onion, diced
5 eggs
1 ½ cups cheddar, shredded

1. Preheat oven to 375 degrees.
2. In a large mixing bowl combine the ground pork, mustard, sage, rosemary, salt, white pepper and garlic powder to make the sausage. Mix well.
3. Saute the sausage and onion over high heat until browned.
4. In a separate mixing bowl beat the eggs and stir in the cheese.
5. Mix the egg and cheese with the browned sausage and pour into a lightly buttered 9×13 casserole dish and bake for 20 minutes. Cool for 5 minutes before serving.

COOK'S NOTE
Say goodbye to all those food additives and make your own pork sausage.

SWEET & SPICY STIR-FRY

A quick and easy stir-fry with a delicate sweet flavor.

Serves 2
Oxalate Content Per Serving: 9.17 mg

INGREDIENTS
2 tbsp. coconut oil
½ yellow onion, thinly sliced
½ red bell pepper, thinly sliced
2 boneless chicken breast fillets, cut into ¾ inch pieces
2 garlic cloves, crushed
½ tsp. white pepper
4 cups napa cabbage, chopped
4 tbsp. rice wine (may substitute with any dry white wine)
5 tsp. coconut sugar
Cooked white rice (optional)

1. Heat the wok or skillet over high heat and add the coconut oil.
2. When the oil is heated, add onion and bell pepper and cook until tender.
3. Add the cut up chicken and stir-fry for about 3 minutes. (Cut a piece to make sure it's not pink inside.)
4. Season with garlic, and white pepper.
5. Add the cabbage and continue to stir-fry, for about 8 minutes, until it starts to brown and stick to the skillet.
6. Reduce the heat to medium-high. Add the wine and the coconut sugar and stir-fry for another minute to blend the flavors.
7. Transfer to a serving dish, and serve hot or over cooked rice. Adding 1 cup cooked white rice will also add 2.40 mg of oxalate per serving.

PIZZA CASSEROLE

This recipe is like a deep dish pizza with an amazing flourless crust.

Serves 8
Oxalate Content Per Serving: 1.19 mg

INGREDIENTS
CRUST
4 oz. cream cheese, softened
2 eggs
¼ tsp. garlic powder
2 oz. Parmesan cheese, shredded
8 oz. mozzarella cheese, shredded
1 tbsp. coconut oil

TOPPINGS
½ onion, diced
½ red or yellow pepper, diced
1 lb. ground grass-fed beef (or turkey, venison, bison)
1 garlic clove, chopped
4 oz. mozzarella cheese, shredded
4 oz. Parmesan cheese, shredded

1. Preheat oven to 400 degrees.
2. In a medium-size bowl, blend the softened cream cheese with the eggs and garlic until smooth and creamy.
3. Stir in the Parmesan and mozzarella until it's all moistened.
4. Spread the crust mixture evenly in a well oiled 9×13 inch glass or ceramic baking dish.
5. Bake 20-25 minutes until evenly browned.

6. In a large nonstick skillet or wok, heat the coconut oil and stir-fry the diced onion and pepper, for about 3 minutes, until soft.
7. Add in the beef and garlic. Cook until done.
8. Add any additional pizza toppings as desired.
9. Spread the meat and vegetables over the cooked pizza crust and top with the mozzarella and Parmesan cheeses.
10. Bake for about 5 minutes or until the cheese is melted.
11. Let it stand for about 5 minutes; then cut and serve squares.

COOK'S NOTE
One serving of this hearty pizza supplies 52% of your daily requirement for vitamin B12 and 44% of your daily requirement for calcium.

MAPLE GLAZED CHICKEN

This flavorful dish is has a tangy and sweet glaze that coats the tender roasted chicken.

Serves 4
Oxalate Content Per Serving: 1.25 mg

INGREDIENTS
4 chicken thighs
4 tbsp. butter
¼ cup maple syrup
¼ cup water
¼ cup white wine vinegar
¼ 4 tsp. salt
½ tsp. white pepper
3 garlic cloves, minced
¼ cup yellow onion, diced
¼ cup red bell pepper, diced
1 tsp. Tabasco sauce
2 tsp. cornstarch

1. Preheat the oven to 450 degrees.
2. Oil a 9×12 ceramic or porcelain casserole dish and add the chicken.
3 In a small saucepan, mix and heat the remaining ingredients except the cornstarch.
4. Whisk the cornstarch in a tsp. of water and then blend in a small amount of the warm sauce. Slowly add the cornstarch mix to the saucepan.
5. Bring to a simmer and then pour the sauce over the top of the chicken.
6. Bake for 30 minutes then turn the oven to broil and set dish under the broiler for about 5-6 minutes.

COOK'S NOTE
Chicken thighs are an excellent source of many essential nutrients, especially iron and zinc which are important for a healthy immune system.

The sap of the sugar maple tree is one of the most delicious natural and healthy sweeteners in the world. Be sure to purchase real maple syrup and not the corn or sugar based pancake syrups.

BIEROCK SKILLET

Bierock Skillet is the American version of the German recipe called Bierock. It's simply ground beef, onions and cabbage.

Serves 4
Oxalate Content Per Serving: 3.23 mg

INGREDIENTS
3 tbsp. butter
1 medium yellow onion, chopped
1 lb ground beef
1 head napa cabbage, chopped (about 4 cups)
¼ cup water

1. Heat the butter in a large skillet and then stir fry the onion until soft.
2. Add in the beef and stir fry until done.
3. Add in the chopped cabbage with ¼ cup water and stir the ingredients until cabbage is cooked.

COOK'S NOTE
This recipe is a rich source of vitamins A, K and C, potassium and iron.

COCONUT CRUSTED COD

The mild, delicate flavor of cod is enhanced with this crispy sweet coconut crust.

Serves 4
Oxalate Content Per Serving: 0.80 mg

INGREDIENTS
4 tbsp. cornstarch
¼ tsp. salt
1 egg
1 tbsp. honey
½ cup unsweetened coconut, shredded
3 tbsp. coconut oil
4 wild-caught (fresh or frozen) codfish filets, thawed and patted dry

1. In a shallow mixing bowl or plate, blend the cornstarch and salt together.
2. In a separate shallow mixing bowl, beat the egg, add the honey and mix well.
3. Spread the coconut out on another plate.
4. In a large nonstick skillet, heat oil over medium-high heat.
5. Set the fish fillets in the cornstarch and pat off the excess then coat with the egg.
6. Press both sides of the fish into the shredded coconut.
7. Cook on one side to a light golden brown for about 3 minutes. Then turn and cook an additional 2-3 minutes. (If the fillets are thick you might need to reduce the heat and cook another 2-3 minutes.) Serve hot.

LOW OXALATE BURRITO

Black-eyed peas create the tasty filling for these homemade wraps.

Serves 2
Oxalate Content Per Serving: 1.58 mg

INGREDIENTS
2 GRAIN-FREE WRAPS
1 tbsp. cornstarch
1 tbsp. coconut flour
1 pinch salt
1 lg. egg
3 ½ tbsp. milk

FILLING
1 cup cooked black-eyed peas
½ tsp. garlic powder
2 tbsp. yellow onion, chopped
1 cup cheddar cheese, shredded
2 tbsp. sour cream

1. For the wraps mix the dry ingredients and in a separate bowl whisk the egg and milk.
2. Combine the wet and dry ingredients stirring gently.
3. Lightly oil a skillet and heat to medium-low. Pour ½ the batter into the skillet and move it around to spread it out.
4. Cook for 3-4 minutes then flip and cook another 2 minutes. Transfer to a cooling rack and repeat for the second wrap.
5. Using the same skillet, heat the black-eyed peas, salt and garlic. Mash them with a fork as they heat.
6. Add the peas, cheese, onion and sour cream to each wrap. Fold and serve.

KENTUCKY-STYLE BOURBON CHICKEN

Sophisticated yet simple slow cooker Bourbon chicken thighs are a traditional southern favorite.

Serves 4
Oxalate Content Per Serving: 0.37

INGREDIENTS
2 tbsp. butter
4 chicken thighs
1 tbsp. yellow onion, diced
¼ tsp. garlic powder
¼ cup white wine vinegar
¼ cup maple syrup
¼ cup Bourbon
¼ tsp. salt
¼ tsp. white pepper

1. Spread the butter around the bottom of the slow cooker.
2. Add the chicken.
3. Mix remaining ingredients in a bowl and pour over the chicken.
4. Cook on low for 6-8 hours or on high for 3-4 hours.
5. Serve hot.

COOK'S NOTE
Bourbon imparts a rich, robust flavor to the chicken thighs.

CRISPY GARLIC PARMESAN WINGS

Baked instead of fried, these classic chicken wings are crispy and delicious.

Serves 4
Oxalate Content Per Serving: 2.98 mg

INGREDIENTS
12 chicken wings
1 tsp. salt
½ tsp. white pepper
1 tsp. garlic powder
1 tsp. dried oregano
2 eggs, beaten
¾ cup Parmesan cheese

1. Preheat the oven to 425 degrees.
2. Place the wings in a large bowl and season the with the salt, pepper, garlic powder and oregano.
3. Beat the eggs in a shallow bowl with 1 tbsp. of water.
4. Pour the eggs into the bowl of chicken and mix well.
5. Add in the Parmesan cheese and coat the wings on all sides.
6. Place the chicken wings on a parchment lined baking sheet.
7. Bake for 25-30 minutes.

COOK'S NOTE
If your wings aren't golden and crispy after 30 minutes, turn the broiler on and broil them for about 3 more minutes, watching them carefully as they could burn quickly. The parchment paper can burn as well.

WHITE CHICKEN CHILI

Enjoy a taste of the south with this delicious white chicken chili full of spice, chicken and low oxalate black-eyed peas.

Serves 2
Oxalate Content Per Serving: 5.04 mg

INGREDIENTS
4 tbsp. butter or ghee
2 large chicken breasts, cut into bite-size pieces
2 cloves garlic, chopped
½ yellow onion, diced
½ tsp. salt
1 tsp. white pepper
4 ½ cups black-eyed peas, cooked
1 cup water
1 cup sour cream
4 oz. cream cheese

1. Heat butter or ghee in a large pot over medium heat and add chicken, garlic, onion, salt and pepper.
2. Cook and stir until juices run clear, 5 to 8 minutes. Stir in the cooked black-eyed peas and water.
3. Reduce heat to medium-low and simmer, stirring occasionally, until flavors combine, about 10 minutes.
4. Stir in the sour cream and cheese and simmer until thick, about 25 minutes.
5. Ladle into bowls.

COOK'S NOTE
Black-eyed peas are mild, flavorful and full of protein. One cup of black-eyed peas is low in fat, cholesterol-free and provides more than 30% of the daily recommended amount of fiber.

GLAZED SALMON

Glazed salmon with a perfectly balanced sweet and savory flavor.

Serves 2
Oxalate Content Per Serving: 3.71 mg

INGREDIENTS
3 tbsp. butter or ghee
5 tbsp. honey
1 tbsp. lemon juice
1 garlic clove, minced
¼ tsp. salt
¼ tsp. white pepper
2 tbsp. Bourbon (optional)
1 can (14 oz.) wild-caught Alaskan Salmon

1. Melt the butter or ghee in a large skillet; then add all of the ingredients except the salmon. Cook over medium heat for about 1 minute.
2. Add in the salmon and break it up into bite size chunks. Toss until the salmon is coated in the sauce.
3. Serve as a main dish or over rice.

COOK'S NOTE
Similar to other oily fish like tuna or trout, salmon is rich in omega-3 fatty acids.

BUTTERY BAKED CHICKEN THIGHS

Nothing more flavorful, simple and quick than this one dish. Butter seared and baked boneless chicken thighs.

Serves 4
Oxalate Content Per Serving: 0 mg

INGREDIENTS
4 tbsp. butter
4 chicken thighs
¼ tsp. salt
¼ tsp. white pepper
½ tsp. garlic powder

1. Preheat oven to 400 degrees.
2. In a large cast iron or oven safe skillet heat your butter and season the chicken.
3. Sear each side of the chicken and then place in the oven.
4. Bake 20 minutes for boneless thighs or 30 minutes for bone in thighs.

COOK'S NOTE
The fat and fatty acids in this dish helps you feel full, regulates body temperature, and manages inflammation and blood clotting.

FLOUNDER WITH LEMON BUTTER

Quick and elegant flounder covered in a lemon butter sauce.

Serves 4
Oxalate Content Per Serving: 0 mg

INGREDIENTS
4 fresh flounder fillets (or substitute any white fish)
½ tsp. salt
¼ tsp. white pepper
4 tbsp. butter
Juice of 1 lemon

1. Pat both sides of the fish fillets dry with paper towels and then season them with salt and pepper.
2. Heat the butter in a medium skillet over medium-high heat. Add the fillets to the skillet and cook, without moving, for 2 minutes.
3. Slide a thin metal spatula underneath the fillets and carefully flip each one. If it seems impossible to slip the spatula beneath the fillet and the skillet, remove the skillet from the heat, wait 30 seconds and try again.
4. Cook the fish about 2 minutes more.
5. Transfer the fish to a platter.
6. Squeeze the lemon juice into the skillet and with the skillet still over the heat and scrape up any browned bits stuck to the bottom of the skillet.
7. Spoon the sauce over the fish and serve.

COOK'S NOTE
Flour isn't at all essential for a lovely sear on fish. Just use a good stainless steel or cast iron skillet and butter.

BAKED BUFFALO CHICKEN TENDERS

Baked chicken tenders covered in buffalo sauce are easy, gluten-free and full of rich spicy flavor.

Serves 4
Oxalate Content Per Serving: 2.80 mg

INGREDIENTS
2 pounds chicken tenders
½ stick butter, melted
1 tbsp. Tabasco sauce
1 tsp. paprika
1 tsp. white pepper
1 tsp. garlic powder
½ tsp. salt
2 tbsp. honey
2 tbsp. coconut flour

1. Preheat oven to 350 degrees.
2. Line a ceramic or porcelain casserole dish with chicken tenders.
3. Mix remaining ingredients in a medium sized bowl and pour over the chicken tenders.
4. Bake for 30 minutes.
5. Place under the broiler an additional 5 minutes.
6. Serve with blue cheese or ranch dressing.

COOK'S NOTE
Buffalo chicken contains a variety of vitamins and minerals. These include vitamin A, vitamin B6, vitamin B12, iron, zinc and selenium.

BEEF CONGEE

This Asian porridge can be made using your preferred meat. I made this one using a 3 pound chuck roast that I prepared in the slow cooker. I only used one half of the roast for this recipe.

Serves 4
Oxalate Content Per Serving: 2.73 mg

INGREDIENTS
1 small beef chuck roast (1 ½ lb.)
1 onion, chopped
1 tsp. garlic
½ tsp. salt
½ tsp. white pepper
3 cups water
2 cups of white Jasmine rice, cooked

1. Add the roast, 4 cups of water, garlic, salt, and pepper to a large slow cooker.
2. Cook roast 6-8 hours on high or until it is easy to shred.
3. Remove the roast and the broth to a large stock pot and shred.
4. Add the cooked rice and simmer on low for another 30 minutes. You want the rice to fall apart. Add more water if it thickens to much. You want the consistency of a thick soup.

COOK'S NOTE
Beef congee is a type of savory rice porridge of Asian origin. It's an ancient remedy in traditional Chinese medicine for a troubled digestive system as it's easy to digest and incredibly nourishing.

HOPPIN' JOHN

Whether you call this Hoppin' John, Jambalaya or Black-eyed Pea Gumbo depends on where you come from. Whatever you call it, the combination of black-eyed peas, salt-cured meat, onion, bell pepper, and rice is a southern classic.

Serves 4
Oxalate Content Per Serving: 4.99 mg

INGREDIENTS
4 tbsp. butter
1 medium-size yellow onion, chopped
1 small red bell pepper, finely chopped
6 thick-cut bacon slices or ham, chopped
3 garlic cloves, chopped
½ tsp. white pepper
¼ tsp. Tabasco sauce
1 tsp. salt
2 cups water
4 cups black-eyed peas, cooked
1 ½ cups white Jasmine rice, cooked
Fresh scallions, sliced

1. Heat the butter in a large skillet and cook the onion and bell pepper until soft.
2. Add in the bacon or ham and cook until done.
3. Transfer to a large pot and add the remaining ingredients. Bring to a boil.
4. Remove from heat and serve.

COOK'S NOTE
Black-eyed peas are also known as cowpeas, black-eyed beans, or goat peas. They are rich in fiber and protein, which makes them an excellent energy source.

SUSHI BOWL

A simplified way to enjoy all the flavors of a sushi roll in a fraction of the time.

Serves 2
Oxalate Content Per Serving: 9.74 mg

INGREDIENTS
½ Hass avocado, moderately ripe
½ medium cucumber
4 oz. cream cheese
2 dried seaweed sheets, also known as Nori
2 cups white Jasmine rice, cooked
1 tsp. lemon juice or white wine vinegar
¼ tsp. salt

1. Chop your avocado and cucumber into small bite-size pieces.
2. Cut your cream cheese into strips.
3. Cut or tear the seaweed into small pieces.
4. Once you have everything prepared assemble the bowls in layers. Start with a layer of rice, add the seaweed, more rice, cream cheese, avocado, and then cucumber.
5. Season with lemon juice and salt and serve.

COOK'S NOTE
One sheet of Nori contains the same amount of fiber as a cup of spinach and is loaded in iodine, a mineral essential for proper hormone function.

FRIED SARDINES

Golden brown and crispy, these tender sardines are a tasty quick snack, appetizer or light lunch.

Serves 2
Oxalate Content Per Serving: 3.14 mg

INGREDIENTS
1 can (3-4 oz.) sardines, drained
1 egg
½ cup cornstarch
¼ tsp. garlic powder
¼ tsp. salt
½ tsp. white pepper
¼ cup coconut oil

1. Rinse and place the sardines on a paper towel to dry.
2. Beat the egg in a shallow bowl and set aside.
3. In another bowl, mix together the cornstarch, garlic powder, salt and pepper.
4. Heat the coconut oil in a large frying pan over medium heat.
5. Dip each sardine into the egg, then into the cornstarch to coat both sides and place in the frying pan.
6. Cook the sardines for about 2 minutes; then turn and cook another 1-2 minutes.
7. Remove from the pan and place on a plate. (Do not place on a paper towel or they will lose their crispness). Serve.

COOK'S NOTE
Sardines are an excellent source of vitamin B12, Omega 3, vitamin D and calcium.

CHICKEN PICCATA

Lemony chicken piccata is super quick and easy to make with pounded chicken breasts and a pan sauce made with butter, white wine and lemon juice.

Serves 2
Oxalate Content Per Serving: 1.65 mg

INGREDIENTS
4 tbsp. butter
¼ tsp. salt
¼ tsp. garlic powder
3 tbsp. cornstarch
2 chicken breasts, beaten thin
1 tbsp. olive oil
1 cup water
Juice of 1 lemon
¼ cup white wine
2 tbsp. capers, drained

1. Heat the butter in a skillet.
2. Spread the cornstarch, salt and garlic powder out on plate and lightly touch the chicken on each side to coat. Pat the chicken to remove all but a light coating.
3. Add the chicken to the skillet and cook over medium/high heat until golden brown on each side (about 5-6 minutes).
4. Transfer the chicken to plates.
5. Add the olive oil, water and lemon and wine to the skillet. Stir to pick up the bits left in the skillet.
6. Add in the capers and mash a few to incorporate the flavor into the sauce.
7. Cook for about 3 minutes and then pour over the chicken. Serve with lemon slices.

BAKED GARLIC AND PARMESAN THIGHS

Garlic and Parmesan cheese is a flavor combination that goes well with juicy tender chicken thighs.

Serves 4
Oxalate Content Per Serving: 0.62 mg

INGREDIENTS
4 boneless chicken thighs
4 tbsp. butter
2 cloves garlic, minced
1 tsp. white pepper
½ cup Parmesan cheese, grated or shredded

1. Preheat oven to 400 degrees.
2. In a large mixing bowl add the chicken, melted butter, garlic and white pepper. Coat each thigh evenly.
3. Spread the cheese on a plate and roll each thigh in the cheese to coat.
4. Place each thigh on a parchment lined baking sheet.
5. Bake for 20-25 minutes.

MOCK CHICKEN AND DRESSING

Fresh corn and coconut flour replaces the traditional corn meal for this low oxalate southern favorite dish.

Serves 2
Oxalate Content Per Serving: 3.60 mg

INGREDIENTS
½ yellow onion, chopped
4 tbsp. butter
2 small chicken breasts, cooked and shredded
3 eggs, boiled and chopped

½ tsp. sage
No Cornmeal Cornbread (see page 57)

GRAVY
3 tbsp. cornstarch
1 cup chicken broth
¼ tsp. salt
½ tsp. white pepper

1. Preheat the oven to 400 degrees.
2. Saute the onion in butter.
3. In a large casserole dish add the chicken, onion, eggs, sage and mock cornbread.
4. Lightly mix then press it down and bake for 15 minutes During this time prepare the gravy.
5. In a small bowl or cup, mix the cornstarch and a small portion of the broth.
6. In a small saucepan over high heat add the broth then gradually stir in the cornstarch mix, salt and white pepper.
7. Serve the dressing and the gravy separately.

COOK'S NOTE
Always choose organic corn to avoid glyphosate which interferes with fundamental biochemical reactions and inhibits the growth of beneficial bacteria. It's also been known to convert to oxalates.

SLOW COOKER MUSTARD BARBECUE CHICKEN

This South Carolina style barbecue sauce adds a tangy sweet and spicy flavor to slow cooked chicken breasts.

Serves 4
Oxalate Content Per Serving: 1.68 mg

INGREDIENTS
1 tbsp. coconut oil
2 boneless chicken breasts
¼ cup white wine vinegar
¼ cup maple syrup
¼ cup water
3 tsp. Dijon mustard
2 tsp. mustard
3 garlic cloves, crushed
¼ tsp. paprika
¼ tsp. Tabasco sauce
½ yellow onion, diced
¼ tsp. salt

1. Spread the oil in the bottom of the slow cooker and add the thawed chicken breasts.
2. In a bowl, mix remaining ingredients and pour over the chicken.
3. Cook on low 6-8 hours or on high for 4 hours.
4. Using two forks, shred the chicken mixing it with the sauce.
5. Serve over rice, on a bun, or with your favorite side dish.

COOK'S NOTE
This simple sauce is so delicious you will never be tempted to buy bottled barbecue sauce again.

BAKED BUFFALO WINGS

Easy gluten-free, restaurant-style buffalo wings that are baked instead of fried.

Serves 2
Oxalate Content Per Serving: 2.40mg

INGREDIENTS
8-10 chicken wings
½ cup melted butter
5 oz. Tabasco sauce

1. Preheat oven to 425 degrees.
2. Spread wings out on a parchment lined baking sheet.
3. Bake for 25-30 minutes, turning once.
4. In a large skillet melt the butter, add the Tabasco sauce, then add the cooked wings.
5. Toss until the wings are coated and serve.

COOK'S NOTE
Cook your own buffalo chicken wings instead of using packaged wings which tend to have unhealthy ingredients.

***

SIDE DISHES

COCONUT RICE

Coconut milk lends fat and sweetness to rice, making it a rich mellow side dish.

Serves 2
Oxalate Content Per Serving: 2.19 mg.

INGREDIENTS
1 cup coconut milk (canned, Chaokoh)
1 cup water
1 cup white Jasmine rice, uncooked
1 pinch salt

1. In a medium sized pot, add the coconut milk, water, rice and salt.
2. On high heat, allow the mixture to boil. Once it starts to boil, turn the heat down to low and cook covered for 20 minutes.
3. Fluff and serve.

COOK'S NOTE
Coconut rice is a rich, savory side dish that goes well with Asian and Asian inspired dishes.

MOCK POTATO SALAD

Cooled rice replaces high oxalate potatoes in this delicious mock potato salad that tastes so much like the old classic southern potato salad that you'll not notice the difference.

Serves 2
Oxalate Content Per Serving: 5.23 mg

INGREDIENTS
2 cups white Jasmine rice, cooked and cooled
6 eggs, boiled, peeled and chopped
½ cup dill pickle, chopped
Juice of 1 lemon
1 cup mayonnaise (preferably Hellman's Organic)
1 tbsp. Dijon mustard
1 tsp. salt
Paprika to garnish

1. Prepare the rice and allow it to cool ahead of time. Best if refrigerated overnight.
2. Prepare the eggs and add them to a large serving dish.
3. Add the chopped pickles, lemon juice, mayonnaise, Dijon mustard and salt; then stir in the rice.
4. Garnish with paprika and serve cold.

COOK'S NOTE
The process of cooking and then cooling rice leads to the formation of resistant starch, a type of dietary fiber. Resistant starch helps prevent constipation and prevent DNA damage in colon cells.

SPAGHETTI SQUASH ALFREDO

Spaghetti squash is a healthy, low oxalate substitute for pasta yet every bit of the garlicky, cheesy goodness is still there.

Serves 4
Oxalate Content Per Serving: 1.8 mg

INGREDIENTS
½ medium spaghetti squash, cooked
2 tbsp. butter
1 ½ cup sour cream
¼ tsp. salt
½ tsp. garlic powder
½ tsp. white pepper
1 cup Parmesan cheese, grated

1. In a small saucepan, melt the butter over low heat. Add the sour cream, salt, garlic, white pepper and Parmesan cheese.
2. Cook over medium/low heat for 5-6 minutes until the cheese melts.
3. Add in the spaghetti squash and stir lightly to blend.
4. Serve hot.

COOKS NOTE
This recipe is easiest if you prepare the spaghetti squash ahead of time by pricking it with a paring knife and placing it in a slow cooker on high for 3-4 hours on high. To check if it's done press the squash with a spoon to see if it dents easily. Remove it, allow it to cool then slice it in half and remove the seeds. Scrape the squash away from one half and store the other half in an air tight container in the refrigerator. It will keep for 5-7 days.

CARAMELIZED ACORN SQUASH

A simple, sweet combination of squash, butter and maple syrup is the perfect way to enjoy something sweet but still be a healthy addition to savory dishes.

Serves 2
Oxalate Content Per Serving: 1.78 mg

INGREDIENTS
1 acorn squash, cut in half and seeds removed
2 tbsp. butter
2 tsp. honey
½ tsp. salt

1. Preheat oven to 425 degrees.
2. Place acorn squash on a baking sheet cut side up.
3. Place 1 tbsp. butter and 1 tsp. honey in each acorn half.
4. Sprinkle with salt.
5. Bake for 45-50 minutes or until squash is tender and serve.

COOK'S NOTE
Winter squash is in fact a truly delicious way to squeeze in an extra serving of vegetables. You can't go wrong with this sweet, buttery, dessert-like vegetable.

SPAGHETTI SQUASH CASSEROLE

Silky spaghetti squash topped with seasoned corn and melted cheese.

Serves 6
Oxalate Content Per Serving: 0.89 mg

INGREDIENTS
1 spaghetti squash, cooked
1 cup cheddar, shredded and divided
2 tbsp. butter
1 medium yellow onion, chopped
1 cup corn
¼ tsp. garlic powder
¼ tsp. salt
¼ tsp. white pepper

1. Slice the cooked squash in half and remove the peel and seeds.
2. Line the bottom of a 9×13 casserole dish with the squash and press it down.
3. Top the squash with half of the cheddar cheese.
4. In a large skillet, melt the butter over medium-high heat and cook the onion for about 3 minutes until soft.
5. Add the corn and stir-fry for about 2 minutes (if using frozen corn cook an extra minute).
6. Pour the cooked onion and corn over the squash. Spread it out evenly, and season with garlic powder, salt, and pepper.
7. Top with the remaining cheese and place the dish under the broiler for about 2-3 minutes to melt the cheese.
8. Serve hot.

CREAMY BROCCOLI MASH

A healthy, nutritious dish full of fiber and flavor.

Serves 4
Oxalate Content Per Serving: 2.94 mg

INGREDIENTS
1 head broccoli or 16 oz. frozen broccoli florets
4 tbsp. butter
1 tsp. garlic powder
⅓ cup whole milk yogurt or sour cream
¼ tsp. salt
¼ tsp. white pepper

1. Chop the broccoli into florets or use frozen broccoli florets.
2. Boil the broccoli in plenty of water for 7 minutes. Drain and discard the water.
3. Blend in a food processor or use an immersion blender.
4. Add the butter, garlic, yogurt or sour cream, and salt and pepper.
4. Stir until the butter melts and serve.

COOK'S NOTE
Broccoli is bursting with vitamins and minerals. It's an excellent source of immune-boosting vitamin C, providing over 81 mg, or about 135% of your daily needs. It is also an excellent source of vitamin K, important in bone health and wound healing.

BUFFALO CAULIFLOWER

These low carb and vegetarian buffalo cauliflower bites have a soft and tender inside and crispy outside.

Serves 4
Oxalate Content Per Serving: 1.63 mg

INGREDIENTS
2 tbsp. butter
2 tbsp. Tabasco sauce
2 cups fresh cauliflower florets
2 tbsp. olive oil
½ tsp. salt
½ tsp. garlic powder

1. Preheat the oven to 450 degrees.
2. Line a rimmed baking sheet with parchment paper.
3. In a small saucepan, melt the butter and whisk in the Tabasco sauce. Set aside.
4. In a large bowl, toss the cauliflower florets with the olive oil, salt and garlic powder.
5. Spread on the baking sheet and roast until tender-crisp (about 15 minutes).
6. Switch the oven to broil and set an oven rack about 6 inches below the heat element.
7. Add the roasted cauliflower back to the large bowl and mix in the hot sauce mixture.
8. Return the cauliflower florets to the baking sheet and broil until browned and bubbly, keeping a close eye on them so they don't burn (about 2-3 minutes).

BROCCOLI CHEESE BITES

These baked broccoli cheese bites are an easy, healthy, and delicious snack or side dish.

Serves 12 (2 broccoli bites each)
Oxalate Content Per Serving: 0.95 mg

INGREDIENTS
2 ½ cups broccoli florets
2 eggs, lightly beaten
¼ cup onion, diced
½ cup, Parmesan cheese, grated
¼ cup plain whole milk yogurt or sour cream
1 cup cheddar cheese, grated
1 tsp. lemon juice
½ tsp. salt

1. Preheat oven to 350 degrees.
2. Lightly oil 2 mini muffin pans or use paper muffin cups. If using regular muffin tins, simply use less mix in each cup.
3. Chop the broccoli into bite size pieces and add them to a large saucepan. Cover the broccoli with water and bring to a boil. Turn down the heat and simmer for about 3 minutes.
4. Drain and rinse with cold water to stop the cooking. This also reduces the oxalate content.
5. In a large bowl, mix the remaining ingredients and stir in the broccoli.
6. Divide the broccoli mix into the muffin cups and bake for 25 minutes until cooked through and lightly browned on the top.

COOK'S NOTE
With so many delicious flavors and nutrients, you may want to freeze some extras to serve later for a healthy breakfast or snack. Simply prepare the muffins as directed and let them cool before storing in an airtight container. These bites can be kept in the fridge for 3 days or frozen up to 3 months.

BUTTER BAKED CAULIFLOWER

Butter-roasting infuses cauliflower with a nutty flavor that melts in your mouth.

Serves 4
Oxalate Content Per Serving: 2.78 mg

INGREDIENTS
1 head cauliflower (4 cups), cut into bite-sized florets
½ tsp. salt
¼ tsp. white pepper
¼ cup butter

1. Preheat the oven to 400 degrees.
2. Cut the cauliflower into small florets; the smaller they are the quicker they will be done.
3. Place in a large baking dish and season with salt and pepper.
4. Sprinkle with melted butter.
5. Bake on the upper rack in the oven for about 20 minutes or more, depending on the size of the florets.

COOK'S NOTE
Cauliflower is rich in antioxidants and anti-inflammatory compounds.

BLACK-EYED PEAS

Black-eyed peas are soul food in south. They're incredibly flavorful, creamy and chock-full of richness.

Serves 3
Oxalate Content Per Serving: 1.29 mg

INGREDIENTS
1 cup dried black-eyed peas
2 ½ cups water
½ tsp. salt
½ tsp. white pepper

1. Rinse and sort peas.
2. In a large bowl add the peas and fill the bowl with water. Soak for a few hours or overnight.
3. Drain the peas then add them to a saucepan.
4. Add 2 ½ cups water and bring to a boil.
5. Reduce the heat to low, cover and simmer for 45 minutes.
6. Season with salt and pepper and serve.

COOK'S NOTE
Soaking releases some of the toxic lectins and oxalates which can be drained off.

BLACK-EYED PEA CAKES

These savory cakes are the perfect Southern-inspired appetizer or side dish.

Serves 2
Oxalate Content Per Serving: 3.13 mg

INGREDIENTS
2-3 tbsp. butter or ghee for frying
1 garlic clove minced
½ small yellow onion, diced
½ tsp. white pepper
2 cups black-eyed peas, cooked
1 egg
1 tbsp. olive oil
¼ cup cornstarch
¼ tsp. salt
¼ tsp. white pepper
3 tbsp. Coconut oil

1. In a medium-size skillet, heat 2 tablespoons of butter or ghee. Add the garlic and onion and cook over moderate heat just until softened (about 3 minutes).
2. Add white pepper and 1 cup of the black-eyed peas and mix well.
3. Pour the mixture into the bowl of a food processor and pulse until the mixture is finely chopped but not smooth.
4. Scrape the mixture into a medium bowl and add in the remaining whole black-eyed peas, egg, olive oil, cornstarch and seasonings. Mix well.
5. Form the mixture into twelve ¼ cup patties, about ½ inch thick.
6. In a very large skillet, heat coconut oil and add the cakes. Fry over medium heat until golden brown, for about

2 minutes per side.
7. Drain on paper towels. Serve the black-eyed pea cakes as a side dish.

COOK'S NOTE
Black-eyed peas are high in protein and fiber, along with micro-nutrients such as folate, copper and thiamine.

OVEN ROASTED CABBAGE STEAKS

This crispy, delicious side dish roasts fresh cabbage with garlic elevating this healthy vegetable to a new level.

Serves 4
Oxalate Content Per Serving: 5.31 mg

INGREDIENTS
1 head (4 cups) Savoy cabbage
1 tsp. garlic powder
4 tbsp. butter, melted
Salt and pepper, as desired

1. Preheat oven to 400 degrees.
2. Slice the cabbage into ½ inch thick steaks.
3. Brush with butter on both sides and place onto parchment lined baking sheet.
4. Roast for 17-20 minutes or until caramelized.
5. Salt and pepper as desired.
6. Remove and serve.

COOK'S NOTE
Cook time may have to be adjusted depending on the thickness of the steaks. Cook until tender and brown.

PEAS AND GREENS

Slow cooked black-eyed peas and greens is a great Southern comfort food that is as healthy as it is delicious.

Serves 4
Oxalate Content Per Serving: 5.32 mg

INGREDIENTS
1 ½ cups dried black-eyed peas
5 cups water
2 tbsp. butter
½ red bell pepper, diced
1 medium yellow onion, diced
3 garlic cloves, minced
1 tsp. white pepper
1 medium bok choy, (2 cups) trimmed and chopped
1 tsp. salt.

1. Sort and rinse the black-eyed peas under warm water.
2. Spread the butter in the bottom of the slow cooker.
3. Place all of the ingredients except the bok choy and the salt in a slow cooker.
4. Cover and cook on low for 6-8 hours or on high for 3-4 hours.
5. Add in the bok choy and salt and allow to cook another 15 minutes before serving.

COOK'S NOTE
If using a frozen package of black-eyed peas this can be made on the stove-top following package directions. Simply eliminate the extra water from the recipe and add the remaining ingredients. If using canned black-eyed peas be aware of the oxalate content. (1 cup canned black-eyed peas = 5 mg oxalates.

CRISPY FRIED ONIONS

Cornstarch replaces higher oxalate cornmeal or flour traditionally used to make onion rings. This fried onion recipe is a quick and easy alternative.

Serves 2
Oxalate Content Per Serving: 1.06 mg

INGREDIENTS
2 egg whites
1 tbsp. cornstarch
1 medium yellow onion, sliced into thin half rings
2 tbsp. coconut oil

1. Beat the egg whites and cornstarch until smooth.
2. Add the chopped onion and mix well.
3. Heat the oil in a skillet and stir fry the onions until done.

COOK'S NOTE
Coconut oil is a great choice for frying, mainly because it can withstand high cooking temperature. It's full of fatty acids that your body needs.

BALSAMIC NAPA CABBAGE

An easy to make, quick, healthy fried cabbage with balsamic vinegar.

Serves 4
Oxalate Content Per Serving: 3.47 mg

INGREDIENTS
2 tbsp. coconut oil or ghee
1 medium yellow onion, chopped
3 garlic cloves, minced
4 cups napa cabbage, chopped
2 tsp. balsamic vinegar
¼ tsp. salt
¼ tsp. white pepper
2 tsp. white wine vinegar

1. Heat the oil in a large skillet and cook the onion and garlic over medium heat for about 3 minutes.
2. Add the remaining ingredients and cook until the cabbage is tender (about 6 minutes).
3. Serve hot.

COOK'S NOTE
The leaves of the napa cabbage are rather ruffled and have a wonderful green color on the outside, turning to light green and then yellow on the inside. Its flavor is mild, and it cooks much quicker compared to other cabbages. It contains important antioxidants that help keep inflammation in check.

CREAMED BOK CHOY

Loads of flavor for a quick and simple side dish.

Serves 2
Oxalate Content Per Serving: 8.90 mg

INGREDIENTS
4 tbsp. butter
2 cloves garlic, minced
1 cup heavy whipping cream
1 tbsp. maple syrup
3 cups bok choy, chopped
½ tsp. salt
½ tsp. white pepper

1. Heat butter in a skillet over medium-high heat.
2. Add garlic and cook for 1 minute.
3. Add cream and maple syrup. Bring it to a light boil and simmer for 4-5 minutes in order for the sauce to reduce by a third.
4. Add in the bok choy and bring to a boil for another minute. The sauce should coat the bok choy completely.
5. Season with salt and pepper and serve immediately.

COOK'S NOTE
Bok choy, also called Chinese cabbage, is a member of the Brassica cabbage family. Bok choy is highly nutritious, high in calcium and very low in carbs.

BOK CHOY STIR-FRY

Tender chopped bok choy with a touch of honey gives this quick Chinese stir-fry a mildly sweet flavor.

Serves 4
Oxalate Content Per Serving: 5.04 mg

INGREDIENTS
2 tbsp. coconut oil
½ medium yellow onion, sliced thin
½ red or yellow pepper, sliced thin
2 garlic cloves, chopped
3 cups bok choy, trimmed and chopped
1 tsp. honey
¼ tsp. balsamic vinegar
¼ tsp. white pepper
¼ tsp. salt

1. In a large nonstick skillet or wok, heat the oil over medium-high heat.
2. Add the onion, sliced pepper and garlic.
3. Stir-fry for about 4 minutes until soft.
4. Add in the bok choy, honey, vinegar, white pepper and salt.
5. Cook another 2-3 minutes until greens are wilted and stalks are crisp-tender.
6. Serve hot.

COOK'S NOTE
Bok choy is a type of Chinese cabbage that's very tender and rich in nutrients including omega-3, zinc, vitamin C, and vitamin K. The combination of balsamic vinegar, honey and salt is a healthy alternative to soy sauce.

BAKED MUSHROOM FRITTATA

A simple and flavorsome oven-baked Italian frittata with mushrooms, scallions and Parmesan cheese.

Serves 4
Oxalate Content Per Serving: 1.16 mg

INGREDIENTS
1 tbsp. butter or ghee
2 cups baby bella mushrooms, sliced
8 large eggs
¼ cup plain whole milk yogurt or sour cream
¼ tsp. sea salt
¼ tsp. white pepper
½ cup scallions, chopped
½ cup Parmesan cheese, grated

1. Preheat oven to 400 degrees.
2. Place a 9-inch pie dish in the oven to warm it up.
3. Heat the butter in a large skillet over medium heat and add the mushrooms. Cook the mushrooms until browned and tender and all liquids have evaporated (about 10 minutes).
4. In a medium sized bowl; beat the eggs with the yogurt, salt and pepper.
5. Add the scallions and the cheese, mixing them in with a spatula.
6. Remove the warm pie dish from the oven and brush in a little butter to coat the dish.
7. Transfer the mushrooms to the baking dish. Then pour the egg mixture on top.
8. Return the baking dish to the oven and bake for about 30 minutes until it's golden brown and puffy and a knife inserted in the center comes out clean. Cool before slicing.

COOK'S NOTE
Mushrooms are very low in calories and rich in selenium, copper and all of the B vitamins. They also contain phenols and other antioxidants that provide anti-inflammatory protection.

CAULIFLOWER MOCK POLENTA WITH EGG

A corn-free take on polenta using cauliflower.

Serves 4
Oxalate Content Per Serving: 2.72 mg

INGREDIENTS
4 cups cauliflower, chopped
4 tbsp. butter or ghee
3 cups water
¼ tsp. salt
1 egg, cooked as desired

1. Chop the cauliflower into chunks and pulse the pieces in a food processor. Pulse until all the cauliflower is in very small grain-like pieces.
2. Add butter to a large frying pan. On medium heat add the cauliflower and half of the water.
3. Simmer for about 15 to 20 minutes or until the cauliflower is soft. While it's simmering, add the salt and a bit more water if needed.
4. Serve warm topped with egg cooked as desired.

COOK'S NOTE
Cauliflower is an excellent source of both vitamin C and K.

BUTTERED CABBAGE

A pure and simple side dish loaded with a sweet buttery flavor.

Serves 4
Oxalate Content Per Serving: 5.26 mg

INGREDIENTS
4 cups Savoy cabbage
½ cup butter
¼ tsp. salt
⅛ tsp. pepper

1. Remove outer leaves, cut in half, and remove the core of the cabbage.
2. Halve the sections again and slice the cabbage into thin shreds.
3. In a large nonstick skillet, melt the butter over medium-heat, and then add the cabbage, salt and pepper.
4. Cook for about 5 minutes, stirring occasionally and then cover.
5. Turn the heat down to medium-low and continue to cook for about 5 minutes more or until the cabbage is tender.
6. Serve hot.

COOK'S NOTE
A great accompaniment to pork, beef or chicken. One serving of this buttery cabbage supplies 100% of your vitamin K requirements.

SAUTÉED BRUSSELS SPROUTS

These tiny cabbages simply sautéed with onion create a flavorful one skillet vegetarian dish or can be paired with fish or chicken.

Serves 4
Oxalate Content Per Serving: 7.42 mg

INGREDIENTS
1 tbsp. butter
2 cloves garlic, chopped
½ yellow onion, chopped
¼ tsp. salt
½ tsp. white pepper
½ tsp. dried thyme
1 cup fresh or frozen Brussels sprouts, thawed and halved
½ cup water
1 oz. Parmesan cheese

1. In a large nonstick skillet, heat the butter over medium heat, and then add the garlic and onion. Cook for about 3 minutes until soft.
2. Season with salt, pepper and thyme.
3. Add the halved Brussels sprouts and water and continue to cook over medium heat another 15 minutes with occasional stirring.
4. Serve hot topped with Parmesan cheese.

COOK'S NOTE
Brussels sprouts are high in protein, low in carbohydrate, and are high in vitamins C, K and A.

SAVORY SAVOY SLAW

A tender, tangy, and fresh tasting slaw with a hint of creaminess to bind it together.

Serves 6
Oxalate Content Per Serving: 4.47 mg

INGREDIENTS
4 cups Savoy cabbage
¼ cup white wine vinegar
¼ cup honey
2 tbsp. plain whole milk yogurt
2 tbsp. extra virgin olive oil
½ tsp. salt
¼ tsp. white pepper

1. Slice the cabbage in half through the core. Cut a v-shaped notch around the white core and discard the core. Slice lengthwise into quarters and thinly slice each quarter crosswise into strips.
2. In a medium-size mixing bowl, whisk together the wine vinegar, honey, yogurt, oil, salt and pepper.
3. Pour the dressing over the shredded cabbage. Mix well.
4. Allow to sit for about 15 minutes, stirring occasionally to meld the flavors during this time.
5. Can be served room temperature or chilled.

COOK'S NOTE
Napa or bok choy can also be used in this recipe. Savoy cabbage has the most delicate flavor and a little less crunch.

CORN POLENTA

A simple, smooth, delicious fresh corn polenta to replace high oxalate corn meal or cornflour.

Serves 2
Oxalate Content Per Serving: 1.87 mg

INGREDIENTS
1 ¾ cup organic corn (1 15 oz canned corn, drained)
2 tbsp. whole milk
4 tbsp. butter
1 tbsp. yellow onion, diced
¼ tsp. garlic powder
¼ cup Parmesan cheese

1. Cream the corn and milk in a blender or food processor.
2. Heat the butter and onion in a skillet.
3. Add the corn, season with garlic and cook over medium heat until thickened.
4. Add the cheese and stir until melted.

COOK'S NOTE
Corn is rich in vitamin C and is a good source of the carotenoids, lutein and zeaxanthin, which are good for eye health and help prevent the lens damage that leads to cataracts.

SPICY BOK CHOY SLAW

A quick and easy Asian-inspired side dish that's crunchy and refreshing. Makes the perfect accompaniment to pork.

Serves 2
Oxalate Content Per Serving: 1.76 mg

INGREDIENTS
3 cups bok choy, chopped
¼ tsp. salt
1 tbsp. Dijon mustard
1 tbsp. white wine vinegar

1. Mix all of the ingredients in a medium sized bowl.
2. Allow it to absorb the flavors for a minute or so before serving.

COOK'S NOTE
A cup of shredded raw bok choy has 1.5 grams of carbohydrate. The veggie provides 0.7 grams fiber and less than a gram of naturally-occurring sugar.

CARIBBEAN SLAW

A mayo-free coleslaw that is light, fruity, sweet and refreshingly delicious.

Serves 4
Oxalate Content Per Serving: 6.38 mg

INGREDIENTS
4 cups Savoy cabbage, shredded
2 tbsp. honey
1 tbsp. lemon juice
1 tsp. garlic, minced
1 tsp. Tabasco sauce
1 tbsp. apricot jam
2 tbsp. sour cream or plain whole milk yogurt
¼ tsp. salt
¼ tsp. white pepper

1. Shred the Savoy cabbage.
2. Mix remaining ingredients and pour over the cabbage.
3. Stir and allow to rest a few minutes before serving.

COOK'S NOTE
Cabbage is a natural prebiotic that provides food to bacterial species in the gut including bifidobacteria and lactobacilli. A healthy gut microbiome is crucial for regulating the immune system and overall health.

RICE AND ONION CAKES

Pan fried rice and onion cakes made easy without a batter. These make an excellent replacement for high oxalate hash browns or potato cakes.

Serves 2
Oxalate Content Per Serving: 3.73 mg

INGREDIENTS
1 cup white Jasmine rice, cooked
½ medium yellow onion, finely chopped
1 egg
3 tbsp. cornstarch
½ tsp. parsley
½ tsp. salt
4 tbsp. coconut oil, for frying

1. In a large bowl combine all ingredients.
2 Heat the coconut oil in a large skillet over medium-high heat.
3. When the oil is hot, drop by spoonfuls and press down slightly to form a flat cake. Don't crowd the pan. Fry one side until golden brown for about 5 minutes and flip.
4. Drain onion cakes on paper towels to absorb excess oil.

COOK'S NOTE
Onions are packed with free-radical-fighting antioxidants, which help repair and protect damaged cells in your body.

***
SMOOTHIES AND DESSERTS

CHERRY ICE CREAM

With just 3 ingredients, create what tastes just like old fashioned homemade ice cream

Serves 4
Oxalate Content Per Serving: 1.58 mg

INGREDIENTS
2 cups plain whole milk yogurt
1 ½ cup frozen pitted cherries
2 tbsp. honey

1. Add all ingredients to a food processor and blend until smooth.
2. Pour into a container and freeze.

COOK'S NOTE
Cherries provide vitamin C, antioxidants and anti-inflammatory compounds.

VANILLA WAFERS

These deliciously sweet and buttery coconut flour vanilla cookies are a gluten-free alternative to the classic vanilla wafer.

Serves 4
Oxalate Content Per Serving: 1.76 mg

INGREDIENTS
¼ cup butter, melted
¼ cup maple syrup
2 eggs
1 tsp. vanilla
¼ tsp. baking soda
¼ tsp. salt
½ cup coconut flour

1. Preheat oven to 350 degrees.
2. Mix all ingredients well.
3. Use a large spoon and drop 16-18 cookies on a parchment lined baking sheet.
4. Bake for 15 minutes.
5. Allow to cool before serving.

COOK'S NOTE
This copycat light and crispy recipe for vanilla wafers replace packaged vanilla wafers that contain unhealthy soybean oil and high oxalate wheat flour.

COCONUT PUDDING

A rich and satisfying coconut pudding that can be served warm or cold

Serves 4
Oxalate Content Per Serving: 1.75 mg

INGREDIENTS
7 eggs
¾ cup sugar in the raw
1 can (13.5 oz.) coconut milk
3 tbsp. cornstarch
¼ cup unsalted butter
2 tsp. coconut extract

1. In a large saucepan, whisk the eggs, sugar and cornstarch then add the coconut milk.
2. Whisk continually over high heat until it begins to boil. (The thickness of the pudding at the end of cooking will be the same thickness when it's cooled.)
3. Remove from heat and whisk in the butter a tbsp. at a time. Lastly, whisk in the coconut extract.
4. Pour into 4 serving dishes and cool.

COOK'S NOTE
Coconuts contain significant amounts of fat, but unlike other nuts, they provide fat that is mostly in the form of medium-chain saturated fatty acids. Lauric acid has a variety of health benefits, including antibacterial, antiviral and anti-fungal properties. Coconut milk is lactose-free, so it can be used as a milk substitute for those with lactose intolerance.

LEMON CUSTARD

Bright, tangy and bursting with lemon flavor with a texture that is both delicate and rich.

Serves 2
Oxalate Content Per Serving: 2.08 mg

INGREDIENTS
5 eggs
½ cup raw sugar
¼ cup lemon juice
¼ cup unsalted butter

1. Whisk the eggs in a medium sized saucepan.
2. Add in the sugar and lemon juice.
3. Cook over medium high heat whisking continually for about 6 minutes or until thickened.
4. Remove from heat and whisk in the butter one tbsp. at a time.
5. Pour into glassware and chill.

COOK'S NOTE
Lemons contain about 50 milligrams of vitamin C, which is over half the amount of vitamin C needed in your daily diet. Vitamin C is an antioxidant which helps protect cells from damage.

MICROWAVE CHEESECAKE

Simple, fast and perfect single serving cheesecake without the fuss of a crust.

Serves 1
Oxalate Content Per Serving: 0 mg

INGREDIENTS
1/3 cup cream cheese, softened
1 egg, beaten
1 ½ tsp. vanilla
1 tbsp. raw sugar

1. Mix all ingredients until smooth.
2. Pour into a buttered ramekin or small bowl.
3. Microwave for 2 minutes.
4. Remove and cool for at least 15 minutes.
5. Serve.

COOK'S NOTE
Cream cheese contains a decent amount of vitamin A. This fundamental fat-solvent nutrient is essential to immune health and manages cell-resistant reactions to fight against pathogens and disease.

VANILLA CUSTARD

Custard with delicate texture and light vanilla flavor

Serves 4
Oxalate Content Per Serving: 1.97 mg

INGREDIENTS
1 tsp. vanilla
2 cups whole milk
1/3 cup raw sugar
6 egg yolks
2 tbsp. cornstarch

1. Add the vanilla, milk and sugar to a large saucepan and turn heat to medium.
2. As the milk is warming beat the egg yolks and add the cornstarch. Whisk until smooth.
3. Add ¼ cup of the warm milk to the yolk mix and whisk. Repeat with another ¼ cup of warm milk.
4. Add yolk mix to the saucepan slowly and continue to whisk.
5. Using a wooden spoon or whisk continue to cook on medium heat until it begins to boil. Remove from heat soon as you see a few bubbles. It should be smooth and thick. The texture you have at the end of cooking will be the same after cooling.
6. Pour into 4 (1/3 cup) serving dishes and allow to cool before refrigeration.

COOK'S NOTE
About half of whole milk's fat consists of monounsaturated and polyunsaturated fat and over one-third of it's fatty acids are Omega-3 which means it's got a great balanced composition of healthy fats.

COFFEE CAKE

The perfect cake for coffee lovers and the low oxalate dieter who wants a cake without wheat flour.

Serves 8
Oxalate Content Per Serving: 0.61 mg

INGREDIENTS
½ cup coconut flour
1 tsp. baking soda
1 tsp. baking powder
¼ tsp. salt
5 eggs
4 oz coffee
¼ cup maple syrup
2 tbsp. butter

1. Preheat oven to 425 degrees.
2. Blend all of the ingredients on low speed until smooth.
3. Pour into a buttered loaf pan or silicone loaf bread mold.
4. Bake for 30-35 minutes.
5. Allow to cool before slicing.

COOK'S NOTE
Yes, this coffee cake has many health benefits. It's full of nutrients that boost your metabolism and offers a great alternative to unhealthy and decadent pastries

COCONUT CAKE
A moist, protein and fiber rich cake made with coconut flour. It's just as healthy as it is delicious.

Serves 8
Oxalate Content Per Serving: 2.70 mg

INGREDIENTS
CAKE
6 tbsp. coconut flour
½ tsp. baking soda
¼ tsp. salt
5 eggs
½ cup maple syrup
2 tsp. vanilla
½ cup coconut oil, melted
½ cup unsweetened coconut, shredded

FROSTING
8 oz. cream cheese, softened
2 tbsp. butter, melted
¼ cup plain whole milk yogurt
1 tsp. vanilla
1 cup maple syrup
1 cup unsweetened coconut, shredded

1. Preheat oven to 325 degrees.
2. Oil a 9×13 inch glass or ceramic baking dish.
3. Mix coconut flour, baking soda and salt in a medium-size bowl.
4. In a separate bowl, add the eggs, syrup, vanilla and coconut oil.
5. Pour the wet ingredients into the dry and mix well using an electric blender on the lowest speed until very smooth.
6. Stir in the shredded coconut and pour the batter into the baking dish. Spread evenly.
7. Bake 35 minutes.
8. Use an electric blender to blend all of the frosting ingredients until smooth.
9. Add 1 cup of coconut flakes and mix well with a spoon.
10. Cool before topping it with frosting.

CHERRY VANILLA SMOOTHIE

Naturally sweet frozen cherries and coconut milk blend to make a cold, creamy, delicious and refreshing smoothie.

Serves 2
Oxalate Content Per Serving: 1.76 mg

INGREDIENTS
1 ½ cups frozen pitted cherries
1 ¼ cups coconut milk
½ tsp. vanilla extract
1 cup water

1. Place the cherries, milk, vanilla extract, and water in the blender and blend until smooth.
2. Pour the smoothie into 2 glasses and serve.

COOK'S NOTE
Cherries are a potent source of antioxidants and anti-inflammatory compounds.

EASY CHEESECAKE

A moist and delicious cheesecake with a buttery, cookie-like, coconut flour crust.

Serves 8
Oxalate Content Per Serving: 1.97 mg

INGREDIENTS
CRUST
¾ cup coconut flour
¼ tsp. salt
½ cup butter, melted

1 tbsp. honey
2 eggs

FILLING
4 eggs
½ cup honey
16 oz. cream cheese, softened
1 tsp. vanilla
1½ cups plain whole milk yogurt

1. Preheat oven to 400 degrees.
2. In a large mixing bowl, mix the coconut flour with the salt and set aside.
3. In a separate mixing bowl, blend the butter, 1 tbsp. honey, and 2 eggs.
4. Add the wet ingredients to the dry and mix well.
5. Oil a 10 inch deep dish glass pie plate and press the crust mixture across the bottom and halfway up the sides of the pie dish. Bake 8 minutes.
6. Remove the crust and turn the oven down to 350 degrees.
7. Add the honey, eggs, cream cheese, vanilla, and yogurt to a mixing bowl and blend on low speed until smooth. Pour it into the pie crust and bake for about 55 minutes.
8. Chill an hour or two before serving.

COOK'S NOTE
The coconut flour crust will darken quite a bit and give it a nutty taste.

COCONUT CREAM SNOWBALLS

This creamy, crunchy, no bake coconut dessert is an all natural delight.

Serves 6 (Makes 12 snowballs)
Oxalate Content Per Serving: 1.00 mg

INGREDIENTS
8 oz. cream cheese, softened
3 tbsp. honey
½ tsp. vanilla
½ tsp. coconut flour
1 cup unsweetened coconut, shredded

1. Combine the cream cheese, honey, vanilla and flour. Blend well.
2. Spread some shredded coconut out on a plate, drop a spoonful of batter onto the plate and use both hands to shape the snowball as you coat with shredded coconut. Toss from hand to hand to remove excess coconut.
3. Repeat the process and add shredded coconut to the plate when needed.
4. Refrigerate for an hour before serving.

COCONUT RICE PUDDING

A wholesome, heartwarming dessert with a creamy vanilla base.

Serves 4
Oxalate Content Per Serving: 0.88 mg

INGREDIENTS
1 ½ cups white Jasmine rice, cooked
2 cups milk or coconut milk, divided
¼ cup honey
½ tsp. salt
1 egg
1 tbsp. butter
½ tsp. vanilla
¼ tsp. nutmeg

1. Mix the cooked rice, 1 ½ cups milk, honey and salt. Cook uncovered over medium heat for about 15-20 minutes.
2. Whisk egg and remaining milk in a bowl.
3. Add about 1 cup of the hot rice mixture to the egg while stirring. Add it back to the pan and cook 2 minutes more.
4. Remove from the heat and add the butter, vanilla and nutmeg.
5. Serve warm.

COOK'S NOTE
When made with natural ingredients, rice pudding can be a healthier alternative to other deserts.

CUCUMBER CANTALOUPE SMOOTHIE

A light and refreshing smoothie.

Serves 2
Oxalate Content Per Serving: 3.62 mg

INGREDIENTS
½ cup romaine
1 cucumber
1 cup cantaloupe
Juice of ½ lemon
1 cup water
½ cup ice cubes

1. Place all ingredients in blender and blend until smooth.
2. Serve.

COOK'S NOTE
Stay hydrated with cucumbers and cantaloupe, both contain 96 and 90 percent water.

WHITE CHOCOLATE CHIP COOKIES

America's favorite cookie made gluten-free with coconut flour and made low in oxalates by using white chocolate chips. A light, textured cookie that is simple yet divine.

Serves 4 (Makes 16-18)
Oxalate Content Per Serving: 3.28 mg

INGREDIENTS
¼ cup butter, melted
¼ cup honey
2 eggs
½ tsp. vanilla
½ tsp. baking soda
¼ tsp. salt
½ cup coconut flour
¾ cup white chocolate chips

1. Preheat oven to 350 degrees.
2. Cover a large baking sheet with parchment paper.
3. In a medium-size bowl, mix the melted butter with the honey until smooth; then add in the eggs, vanilla, baking soda and salt. Mix well.
4. Blend in the coconut flour and allow to stand about 1 minute as the coconut flour absorbs the liquid ingredients.
5. Mix in the white chocolate chips, shape spoonfuls into balls and place on the baking sheet.
6. Using a fork, press down each cookie to the desired size. Cookies will not spread out or rise much.
7. Cook 15-16 minutes. The outside of the cookie should be a golden brown color.
8. Slide the parchment paper off onto a counter and cool for 10 minutes before removing to a serving dish.

COOK'S NOTE
Using honey with coconut flour in a cookie recipe gives the perfect dough consistency for an excellent chewy cookie. These are a dream come true for the gluten intolerant and low-oxalate dieter.

WHITE CHOCOLATE CHERRY SQUARES

A simple yet elegant looking dessert of chewy cherries in sweet white chocolate.

Serves 8
Oxalate Content Per Serving: 1.34 mg

INGREDIENTS
1/3 cup coconut oil
2 cups white chocolate chips
1 ½ tsp. vanilla
A pinch of salt
1 cup sweet cherries, pitted and thawed

1. In a medium-size saucepan, melt the coconut oil and chocolate chips over medium-high heat stirring constantly.
2. Remove from heat and blend in the vanilla, salt, and cherries.
3. Pour into an oiled 9×13 glass baking dish.
4. Refrigerate for about an hour before cutting and serving.

COOK'S NOTE
Continually dip a sharp knife in a glass of hot water to cut the squares. Cherries are packed with antioxidants and offer many health benefits.

WHITE CHOCOLATE MOUNDS

Melt in your mouth white chocolate with a sweet gooey, chewy, coconut center.

Serves 6 (Makes 12)
Oxalate Content Per Serving: 3.46 mg

INGREDIENTS
2 cups unsweetened coconut, shredded
¼ cup coconut oil, melted
½ cup honey
1 tsp. vanilla
½ cup plain whole milk yogurt
1 ½ cup white chocolate chips

1. In a large mixing bowl, combine the coconut, oil, honey, vanilla and yogurt.
2. Form 1 ½ inch balls of coconut mix and place in the freezer for 15 minutes.
3. Melt the chocolate using a double boiler. (Make your own double boiler by selecting a small saucepan and a bowl that will fit over it without falling inside. The bowl should dip partially inside the saucepan. Add 1 inch of water to the small saucepan and bring it to a light boil over medium-high heat.)
4. Add the chocolate to the small bowl on top. Stir gently and continuously until melted.
5. Carefully remove the bowl of melted chocolate and transfer to a heat-safe surface.
6. Using 2 forks, dip one ball at a time into the melted chocolate and place on a parchment lined baking sheet.
5. Let chocolate set before serving.

ABOUT THE AUTHOR

Melinda Keen is an author, middle school teacher and certified nutrition consultant. Her published works included *Low Oxalate Fresh and Fast Cookbook: Hope and Help For The Low Oxalate Dieter* (2015), *Real Food Real Results: Gluten-Free Low-Oxalate, Nutrient-Rich Recipes* (2016) *Living Low Oxalate: When Oxalate Rich Foods Destroy Your Health* (2018) and *Tame The Flame Cookbook: Recipes To Reduce Chronic Inflammation* (2019).

Low Oxalate Fresh and Fast Cookbook contains a collection of meals that are perfect for the cook who wants home-cooked, nutritious, fresh food fast. Each recipe is low in oxalates, averaging 40-50 mg daily. *Real Food Real Results* is an original collection of recipes from breakfasts to breads and crackers, main dishes, sides and desserts. *Living Low Oxalate* is an empowering resource for understanding and treating oxalate toxicity. It includes the oxalate influence on chronic disease, food lists, menu ideas and suggested food swaps for living low oxalate. *Tame The Flame Cookbook* is filled with recipes that reduce chronic inflammation, and helpful food lists such as inflammatory foods, high oxalate foods and anti-inflammatory foods.

Follow Melinda Keen online at https://melindakeen.com/

RECIPE TITLE INDEX

BREADS, CRACKERS AND SNACKS	47
Apple Bars	54
Biscuits	49
Buffalo Chicken Cheddar Bites	56
Carnivore Crackers	52
Cheddar Crisps	53
Cheese Biscuits	48
Chicken and Cheese Pizza Crust	58
Coconut Flour Rounds	50
Coconut Loaf Bread	47
Cornstarch and Egg Wraps	55
No Cornmeal Cornbread	57
Soft Dinner Rolls	51
Toasted Coconut Chips	59

BREAKFAST DISHES	61
Buttery Banana Muffins	65
Cloud Bread Cheese Danish	62
Cream of Coconut	61

Ham and Cheese Egg Puffs	66
Sausage	64
Sausage and Egg Muffins	68
SOS	63
Yogurt Pancakes	67
SOUPS, SALADS AND DRESSINGS	**69**
Arugula and Cauliflower Soup	73
Caesar Dressing	80
Chicken Caesar Salad	79
Chicken Noodle Soup	75
Clam Chowder	74
Corn Chowder	71
Egg Drop Soup	76
Honey Mustard Dressing	81
Italian Dressing	81
Ranch Dressing	82
Slow Cooker Chicken Stew	69
Split Pea Soup	72
Vegetable Pasta Salad	77
Vegetable Soup	70
Warm Ham and Egg Salad	78

MAIN DISHES	83
Asian Pork Patties	97
Baked Buffalo Wings	121
Baked Buffalo Chicken Tenders	112
Baked Garlic and Parmesan Thighs	118
Baked Lemon Rosemary Chicken	89
Beef Casserole	84
Beef Congee	113
Beirock Skillet	103
Buttery Baked Chicken Thighs	110
Chicken Marsala	92
Chicken Piccata	117
Coconut Crusted Cod	104
Crispy Garlic Parmesan Wings	107
Flounder with Lemon Butter	111
Fried Sardines	116
Glazed Salmon	109
Ground Beef Stir-Fry	83
Hoppin' John	114
Kentucky-Style Bourbon Chicken	106
Kentucky-Style Bourbon Barbecue Roast	88
Low Oxalate Burrito	105
Maple Glazed Chicken	102
Mock Chicken and Dressing	118

Pizza Casserole	100
Pork Chops in Gravy	91
Pork Chops in Wine and Garlic Sauce	87
Pork Sausage Casserole	98
Salisbury Steak	90
Salmon Pasta Casserole	96
Salmon Scramble	86
Seared Mahi Mahi Salad	94
Slow Cooker Mustard Barbecue Chicken	120
Sweet and Spicy Stir-Fry	99
Sushi Bowl	115
White Chicken Chili	108
Unstuffed Bell Pepper Bowl	85
SIDE DISHES	**122**
Baked Mushroom Frittata	139
Balsamic Napa Cabbage	136
Black-Eyed Peas	131
Black-Eyed Pea Cakes	132
Bok Choy Stir-Fry	138
Broccoli Cheese Bites	129
Buffalo Cauliflower	128
Butter Baked Cauliflower	130
Buttered Cabbage	141

Caramelized Acorn Squash	125
Caribbean Slaw	146
Cauliflower Mock Polenta with Egg	140
Coconut Rice	122
Corn Polenta	144
Creamed Bok Choy	137
Creamy Broccoli Mash	127
Crispy Fried Onions	135
Mock Potato Salad	123
Oven Roasted Cabbage Steaks	133
Peas and Greens	134
Rice and Onion Cakes	147
Sauteed Brussels Sprouts	142
Savory Savoy Slaw	143
Spaghetti Squash Alfredo	124
Spaghetti Squash Casserole	126
Spicy Bok Choy Slaw	145
SMOOTHIES AND DESSERTS	**148**
Cherry Ice Cream	148
Cherry Vanilla Smoothie	156
Coffee Cake	154
Coconut Cake	154
Coconut Cream Snowballs	158

Coconut Pudding	150
Coconut Rice Pudding	159
Cucumber Cantaloupe Smoothie	160
Easy Cheesecake	156
Lemon Custard	151
Microwave Cheesecake	152
Vanilla Custard	153
Vanilla Wafers	149
White Chocolate Cherry Squares	162
White Chocolate Chip Cookies	161
White Chocolate Mounds	163

Printed in Great Britain
by Amazon